DATE			

Passion and the Passion

PASSION
AND
THE PASSION

Sex and Religion in Modern Literature

by
FRANCIS L. KUNKEL , 1921-

THE WESTMINSTER PRESS
Philadelphia

Copyright © 1975 The Westminster Press

All rights reserved—no part of this book may be reproduced in any form without permission in writing from the publisher, except by a reviewer who wishes to quote brief passages in connection with a review in magazine or newspaper.

Book Design by Dorothy Alden Smith

Published by The Westminster Press®
Philadelphia, Pennsylvania

PRINTED IN THE UNITED STATES OF AMERICA

Library of Congress Cataloging in Publication Data

Kunkel, Francis Leo, 1921–
    Passion and the passion.

    Includes bibliographical references.
    1. Fiction—20th century—History and criticism.
    2. Sex and religion in literature. I. Title.
    PN3503.K8   823′.03   75–20085
    ISBN 0–664–24778–4

To my son

Acknowledgments

I owe a debt to Joseph Cosenza and William Thierfelder, two graduate assistants at St. John's University in New York, for their help with matters of documentation.

Two chapters appeared previously, in somewhat altered form, and are used here by permission of the editors. Chapter 4 appeared in *Commonweal*, February 23, 1968. Chapter 7 appeared in *Continuum*, Spring 1965.

Permission to quote excerpts from copyrighted works has been granted by the following publishers:

Farrar, Straus & Giroux, Inc., for excerpts from works by Flannery O'Connor: *Everything That Rises Must Converge*, copyright © 1956, 1957, 1958, 1960, 1961, 1962, 1964, 1965 by the Estate of Mary Flannery O'Connor; *Mystery and Manners*, copyright © 1957, 1961, 1963, 1964, 1966, 1967, 1969 by the Estate of Mary Flannery O'Connor, copyright © 1962 by Flannery O'Connor, copyright © 1961 by Farrar, Straus and Cudahy, Inc.; *The Violent Bear It Away*, copyright © 1955, 1960 by Flannery O'Connor; *Wise Blood*, copyright © 1949, 1952, 1962 by Flannery O'Connor.

Grove Press, Inc., for numerous selections from *Our Lady of the Flowers*, *Thief's Journal*, *Miracle of the Rose*, and *Funeral Rites*, © 1963 by Grove Press (*Our Lady of the Flowers*), copyright 1964 by Grove Press (*Thief's Journal*), copyright 1966 by Grove Press, translation copyright 1965 by Anthony

Blond, Ltd. (*Miracle of the Rose*), copyright 1969 by Grove Press (*Funeral Rites*).

Harcourt Brace Jovanovich, Inc., for excerpts from *The Spire*, by William Golding, © 1964 by William Golding.

Alfred A. Knopf, Inc., for excerpts from *The Poorhouse Fair*, by John Updike, copyright © 1958 by John Updike, and *Couples*, by John Updike, copyright © 1968 by John Updike.

New Directions Publishing Corporation, for excerpts from *Miss Lonelyhearts* and *The Day of the Locust*, by Nathanael West. Copyright 1933 by Nathanael West, © 1960 by Laura Perelman.

The Viking Press, Inc., for excerpts from *The Collected Letters of D. H. Lawrence*, ed. by Harry T. Moore. Copyright © 1962 by Angelo Ravagli and C. M. Weekley, Executors of the Estate of Frieda Lawrence Ravagli. All rights reserved.

Religion . . . like the open doorway in a red-lamp district led inevitably to sex.

GRAHAM GREENE
A Burnt-Out Case

Contents

Introduction   13

1 Lawrence's *The Man Who Died:*
    The Heavenly Cock   37

2 Golding's *The Spire:*
    The Prayer and the Phallus   58

3 John Updike: Between Heaven and Earth   75

4 Tennessee Williams: God, Sex, and Death   99

5 Jean Genet: Counterfeit Saint   108

6 Wrestlers with Christ and Cupid   129

7 The Sexy Cross   157

Conclusion   169

Notes   185

Index   201

Introduction

Love appears to some as a thoroughly natural and all-pervasive force driving human beings to seek sexual union. Others, agreeing with the all-pervasiveness but not seeing it as an exclusively natural force, add a supernatural element to the definition of love. These age-old, traditionally different outlooks constitute the hedonistic ethos and the religious ethos and still have their respective champions. Federico Fellini, in the course of an interview granted at the premiere of his film *Fellini's Satyricon,* said his intention is "to show that sex is not such a big problem as Christianity has made it. Sex is only the lure of the sexes; sex is just sex."[1] The film, by glorifying a remote hedonistic past, implicitly criticizes the proximate puritanical past and revels in the hedonistic present. Conversely, Malcolm Muggeridge, in a recent book, implies the need for a theology of sex, combining mystery, responsibility, and celebration, when he derides the attitude that sex is just sex. "Sex is the mysticism of a materialist society, with its own mysteries—this is my birth pill; swallow it in remembrance of me!"[2] Later, in the same book, he insists that sex must be seen in the wider context of ethics. "The purpose of it is procreation, the justification of it is love; if you separate sex from procreation and love, very rapidly you turn it into a horror."[3]

One important aspect of the theological ethos as it pertains to twentieth-century literature is the concern of this book. I examine the work of some outstanding writers of the twentieth century who have wrestled either with the significance of Christ or with some other aspect of religion and then coupled their concern with the mystery of sex. In those writers where it is most pronounced, I have isolated this phenomenon in order to investigate their implicit views on the relation of sex to religion. What I have analyzed is certain fictive situations and especially certain characters in which allusions to the erotic occur in a spiritual context and vice versa. It seems curious to me that this equation of spirituality with sexuality—and its corollary, the neo-Christ figure drenched in erotic turbulence, violence, and romantic agony—is so widespread in contemporary literature and yet has received no adequate critical attention. I hope the oversight has been corrected by my concentration on a selected group of modern writers who, in the course of rejecting the hedonistic ethos, confuse—or at least expose themselves to the danger of confusing—the two kinds of love, earthly *amor* and heavenly *caritas*. The body of the work consists of reflections on the sexual implications of religious imagery and the religious implications of sexual imagery. The conclusion pulls the separate studies together for an overall view of the relevant imaginative patterns.

The frequent confusion displayed by the writers under consideration is wrought by the way they mount a passion play on stage, while the Passion play is going on off stage, or vice versa. When you use sex as though it were an accessory to religion or religion as though it were an accessory to sex, you flirt with a heady but potentially explosive combination, eschatology and erotology. This theological-erotic compound, often with scatology added, is to be found in much of the literature of this century. It is polymorphically present to varying degrees in those authors, like Graham Greene, who eagerly search for the sexual implications of spirituality, as well as in those, like Jean Genet, who reluctantly search for the spiritual implications of sexuality. These authors, Christian and otherwise, are working in a new Gothic tradition substituting sexual aberration for ghosts as an accompaniment to religion.

The current trend of canonizing sex as religious expression is not confined to literature, to be sure. It is a cultural craze permeating such diverse areas as the cinema, sociological journals, and group therapy. Andy Warhol combines a well-intoned Kyrie with naked seductions in *Lonesome Cowboys; Easy Rider* mixes sex movingly with requiem and rosary in a New Orleans cemetery. The May 1971 *Evergreen Review* features a piece proclaiming an ecclesiastical function for pornography. "The High Church of Hardcore will have to be invaded by the sanctifying grace of art and truth."[4] And a group in Greenwich Village is sponsoring ritualized orgies "to achieve sexoreligious results." But these popular manifestations are an aside, for I am concerned exclusively with the symbiosis between sex and religion in twentieth-century belles-lettres.

What must first be established by way of necessary background material, however, is that there is nothing new in this nexus. Sex and ritual, sex and faith, sex and mystical union, sex and salvation: these relationships have been part of the implicit wisdom of nearly all religions, even the most primitive. As Andrew Greeley points out: "The ecstatic, primordial, contemplative, ceremonial, ritualistic, communitarian and sexual are words that can be predicative of almost any religious *liturgy* that the human race has observed." He adds that "sex and religion are the two most powerful non-rational forces of the human personality," and so it is not surprising "that they should be linked." The term "non-rational," more applicable at first glance to "the infra-rational of sensualistic orgy," is also applicable to religion in the sense of "the supra-rational of mysticism and contemplation." As evidence of sexual imagery in his own faith, Roman Catholicism, he offers "the intercourse symbol of the candle and the water on Holy Saturday, for example, or the pervasive comparison of the Church to marriage in both the Old and the New Testament."[5]

Although religion and sex, in view of their diverse *raison d'êtres,* would appear to have little to do with each other, this, we see, has not at all been the case. Since the beginnings of early man in Europe, the two have been intimately connected. The modern fiction writers who combine erotica and theology are working in an ancient tradition. The tradition should be surveyed briefly if we are to understand the strong appeal this affinity has for them. The survey, of necessity, will have to be highly selective and confined largely to the Judeo-Christian culture, with only a couple of references outside that pale. Inasmuch as the writers studied are all products of the Judeo-Christian culture, stress on that culture is in order.

Since my intent is literary, it might be well to begin by referring to the ancient Sumerians, the people with the oldest known written language. In a controversial study of their religious practices, entitled *The Sacred Mushroom and the Cross,* John Allegro argues that a universal phallic cult lies at the heart of all religions. "If rain in the desert was the source of life, then moisture from heaven must only be a more abundant kind of spermatozoa. If the male organ ejaculated this precious fluid and made life in the woman, then above the skies the source of nature's semen must be a mighty penis, as the earth that bore its offspring was the womb. It followed therefore that to induce the heavenly phallus man must stimulate it by sexual means, by singing, dancing, orgiastic displays, and above all by performing the copulatory act itself."[6] He goes on not very convincingly to assert that this union of fertility rite and imitative magic influenced the Bible and still influences the religious consciousness of Christians. As Allegro tells it, the Sumerians (ca. 2500 B.C.) were a mushroom-worshiping sect: the sacred mushroom representing the semen implanted on earth by the "mighty penis." He then traces Judaism and Christianity back to the mushroom cult of Sumer, by way of folklore links between the mushroom and the serpent. "The whole Eden story is mushroom-based mythology." In substantiation, he points to the sexual characteristics of the abundant mushroom imagery in the Bible and identifies Eden with the "Garden of Sex." He fantasizes an explanation of Christian origins in which Jesus is "the semen that saves," and Peter is a name derived from the Aramaic word *pitra,* "mushroom." The New Testament, he concludes, deserves to be treated as outright myth with no historical foundation.

But this alliance is a misalliance. To explain Christian origins in terms of a phallic onslaught and to conclude that the actual stories about Jesus are no more real historically than those about Adam and Eve is to ignore historical evidence to the contrary. What the New Testament relates can be checked against other contemporary sources, at least in part, so that it cannot be dismissed as myth. Besides Allegro's credentials as a scholar in this area, his whole argument and even his right to carry on the discussion have been called into question by the eminent Sumerologist, J. S. Cooper, who, prior to citing chapter and verse, makes this allegation. "Dr. Allegro, who is a Qumran (Dead Sea scrolls) specialist and not a Sumerologist, has seen fit to construct his theories upon a foundation of garbled, misinterpreted, or even nonexistent Sumerian words. While I am intrigued to see this obscure and difficult language, with which I do daily battle in the course of my researches, associated with items as exciting and modish as phallic worship and psilocybin, to say that Allegro should have known better would be an understatement."[7] The exposure of the serious shortcomings in Allegro's book is not intended, of course, to discredit fact: the existence of phallocentric religions. That would work against the thrust of my thesis. It is intended to discredit the specific charge that for two thousand years Christians have been worshiping a sacred mushroom without knowing it as well as the general charge that most religious sects are obsessed with the phallus.

Phallic worship was practiced by most of the people with whom the ancient Israelites came into contact. Israel's neighbors, near and far—the Babylonians, the Assyrians, the Canaanites, and the Egyptians—were devoted to polytheistic nature cults that, celebrating fertility and bound to the cyclical rhythms of the seasons of the year, were rife with phallic symbols. Images of Osiris, an Egyptian god, as a bull or with a triple phallus, for example, were displayed in religious processions. According to William Cole, in *Sex and Love in the Bible*, these pagan gods and goddesses were "pictured in the myths and legends as creating the world by copulation. . . . Their worship apparently required a kind of imitative magic in which male and female devotees yoked their bodies sexually and spilled their seed upon the fields they desired to yield bounteous crops."[8] These pagans also practiced sacred prostitution at one of the temples dedicated to a deity. Regarding the form it took in Babylon, Herodotus provides this account: "The foulest Babylonian custom is that which compels every woman of the land once in her life to sit in the temple of Aphrodite and have intercourse with some stranger. . . . After their intercourse she has made herself holy in the goddess's sight and goes away to her home."[9]

Even the Greeks and the Romans, the most civilized pagans, trafficked in religion and sex. Like those of their primitive predecessors, Greek and Roman myths swarm with stories of copulating deities: Zeus and Leda, Zeus and Ganymede, Diana and Endymion, Venus and Adonis, Cupid and Psyche. Studies of Roman sepulchral art indicate the frequency of mythological scenes of love between gods or goddesses and youths or maidens on sarcophagi. Psyche and Cupid united in an embrace and kiss was the most popular funerary symbol of this type. But the gods were not always in a caressing mood; often they demanded stern sacrifice of their human subjects. *The Golden Bough* tells us that the worship of Cybele involved wild and frenzied dances during which the priests of the cult castrated themselves and flung their genitals upon the altar of their goddess.

And in the androgynous myth that he weaves into the *Symposium,* Plato ascribes the need for a partner in sexual intercourse to the indignation of the gods. Aristophanes, an interlocutor, explains that the first human beings were sexually self-sufficient. They possessed the organs of both sexes, until they fell into disfavor with the gods, on account of pride, and were rent in twain. Since the substitution of unisexuality for bisexuality, the dream of every lover is that he should melt into his beloved. "This becoming one instead of two was the very expression of his ancient need. And the reason is that human nature was originally one and we were a whole, and the desire and pursuit of the whole is called love."[10] And while it is a questionable interpretation, the comparative speculation of Nicholas Perella on this point is not without interest. "It is worthwhile remembering that in Genesis, Judaism and Christianity had an androgyne myth also. Both versions of the Genesis account (1:27–28; 2:21–24) of the creation of man consider the original man to be androgynous or hermaphroditic."[11]

Any allusion, even the faintest, to the union of religion and sex in the Old Testament must center on Hosea, the Hebrew prophet in the eighth century B.C. who married a whore. At the command of God, Hosea married Gomer, "a wife of harlotry" (Hos. 1:2). After she was repeatedly unfaithful, he reluctantly sold her into slavery. But so great was his love for her that he bought her back, and they became reconciled. In this turbulent marriage, the anguished prophet saw an analogy between his own long-suffering relationship to his wife and that of God to Israel. As Hosea cast off Gomer for repeated adulteries, so would God cast off Israel for repeated idolatries—symbolic adulteries. But both would recant: as Hosea could not forsake his beloved wife, so God would not forsake his chosen people. The analogy that Hosea saw between a man's sensual love and God's spiritual love is a recurrent metaphor in the Old Testament. The Song of Songs is the most celebrated example.

As Hosea in the Old Testament saw his own marriage to Gomer in terms of the union between God and Israel, so Paul in the New Testament saw marriage in equally mystical-erotic terms. "Husbands, love your wives, as Christ loved the church and gave himself up for her" (Eph. 5:25). The Pauline text coincides with the Hosaic view—human sexuality as a "mystery" analogous to divine love—and exalts matrimony to a new state of sanctity. The conjugal union is not to be wholly sensual, as with the heathens, but rather self-renunciatory for the sake of the spouse, even as Christ gave himself to and for the church. In spite of this, Paul expressed the wish that all Christians were as he, unmarried (I Cor. 7:7). And marital sex is to be primarily for the extrinsic glory of God: less for procreation, least for pleasure. Premarital and extramarital sex are anathema. His initial endorsement of marriage is somewhat offset then by a personally negative attitude toward sex. But it is important to understand the source of Paul's prejudice. As Cole explains: "Paul was no Gnostic, no Hellenistic dualist, counseling asceticism and self-denial out of contempt for the body. His advice about marriage was set against the background of what he called 'the impending distress . . . the appointed time has grown very short . . . the form of this world is passing away' (I Cor. 7:26–31). Paul believed firmly that the end of the world was at hand and that the end would be preceded by a time of troubles in which 'the man of lawlessness, the son of perdition' would reign and rage. Therefore, the fewer earthly concerns binding any Christian, the freer he would be, the more single-minded he would prove in the day of decision."[12] It is just because Paul regarded the body as sacred that he enjoined the Corinthians not to patronize prostitutes. "Know you not that your bodies are the members of Christ? Shall I then take the members of Christ, and make them the members of a harlot? God forbid. . . . Glorify and bear God in your body." (I Cor. 6:15–20.)

It is dubious that Jesus shared the sentiment that sins of the flesh are the worst of sins or agreed with his apostle's dictum: "Do not associate with them [fornicators]" (Eph. 5:7). For Jesus befriended Mary Magdalene, defended the woman taken in adultery, and reserved his ultimate condemnation for the proud and self-righteous Pharisees. And if his miracle at the wedding feast of Cana is any criterion, he approved of marriage, unlike Paul, who, for all his exalted analogies, tolerated it. "Let them marry—it is no sin." (I Cor. 7:36.) "It is better to marry than to be aflame with passion." (I Cor. 7:9.) (If the bulk of the remarks in this paragraph and the foregoing appear to be anti-Pauline, I ask the reader's forbearance until the conclusion where I redress the matter by expressing an entirely pro-Pauline sentiment.)

However, it is unlikely that Jesus' practice with regard to celibacy was at variance with Paul's, despite a heretical tradition to the contrary—a tradition alleging that Jesus loved women in an other than spiritual way. Perella calls our attention to "the early Gnostic text (Gospel of Philip) which spoke of Mary Magdalene as the consort of Christ . . . and . . . early depictions of the Magdalene embracing the foot of the cross," culminating in "the daring conception of Auguste Rodin's sculpture in the late nineteenth century. Rodin depicts a sensuously nude Magdalene literally embracing Christ on the cross and swooning away. It is quite more blatantly sexual than anything in the Baroque age, or at least it fails to show that spiritualization of the sensual that the best Baroque art achieves in its sensuous interpretation of religious ecstasy."[13]

Current speculation on the sexuality of Jesus has its popular (*Jesus Christ Superstar*) and scholarly manifestations. Only the latter, a book by William Phipps (*Was Jesus Married?*), need detain us. Phipps states that Jesus' spouse was Mary Magdalene. He is anxious to show that "if Jesus blessed marriage by personal practice as well as by lofty tribute . . . this should encourage a more healthy climate of opinion toward erotic passion."[14] This is a laudable ambition, but unfortunately Phipps's evidence is less impressive than his ambition. The tardy posting of the nuptials is based largely on studies revealing "not a single instance of life-long celibacy recorded anywhere in the records of Palestinian Judaism." Since this is erroneous, however—the Talmud, cornerstone of Palestinian Judaism, celebrates the celibacy of Rabbi Simon Ben Azzai, sage who flourished during the first third of the second century, on three widely separated pages—and since there is not a shred of evidence in the New Testament or in the early Christian writers that can be invoked to prove that Jesus was married, the assertion has not been taken seriously.

The traditional argument for a celibate Jesus rests upon his own words. "There are eunuchs born that way from their mother's womb; there are eunuchs made so by men, and there are eunuchs who made themselves that way for the sake of the Kingdom of Heaven. Let anyone accept this who can." (Matt. 19:12.) Had the preacher of "the Kingdom" been married, the words would have sounded woefully hollow to the ears of his reluctant listeners. Still, the New Testament affirms that Jesus was tempted in every respect as we are, so doubtless he had sexual desire. But the acceptance of this side of Jesus' humanity does not invalidate the conclusion that he freely chose celibacy and gloriously sublimated those desires in the work of the redemption. The holiness of marital sexuality is not diminished thereby: it depends not upon his personal practice but upon his having ordained marriage as a sacrament. After all, Jesus did not receive some of the other sacraments either, and that does not detract from their efficacy. His freely chosen celibacy amounted to a decision to hallow one of two pagan practices where divinity and sexuality are concerned. Jesus chose to follow the way of the vestal virgins and of the celibate priests of Jupiter and to reject the aforementioned concept of deity copulation.

Sex was sanctified by Christ in terms of the sacraments he instituted, if not by the doctrine of the virgin birth. The sacraments are the channels through which the holy enters life and sanctifies it in its most elementary functions—birth, adolescence, vocation, death, on one plane; sin and amendment, eating, drinking, and sexual intercourse, on another. These great rites of passage common to all folk religions were uniquely blessed by Christ. But the virgin birth set sex back. The impregnation of a virgin by a divine being in the guise of a bird, the issue of which will be another divine being, is exclusively a pagan notion, taken literally. The fulfillment of the Annunciation is unique. What differentiates it from the myth of Zeus and Leda, for example, is the mode of conception, the employment of metaphor. Apart from the swan disguise used by Zeus, the impregnation of Leda took place in the normal way, by penile-vaginal intercourse. Contrary to this, Roman Catholic theology has always insisted on the virginity of the mother of Christ. The traditional teaching is that the Holy Spirit miraculously deposited the divine seed in Mary's womb, so that Jesus came through the maidenhead of the Blessed Virgin as light through glass. Even the most liberal theologians today are less troubled by the virgin birth than by the infallibility of the pope, for instance. Perhaps it is easier to believe in an outright mystery.

The inescapable result of this miracle is to deny that Christ was begotten by seminal ejaculation, as though this would have tainted the Godhead. The accompanying exaltation of virginity and celibacy sets an ascetical tone for the writings of the early church fathers. Beginning with Paul, as we have seen, there was a deep-seated suspicion of sex, despite his claim that the best image to represent Christ and the church is the union between husband and wife. Following Paul, Augustine displayed an ambivalent attitude toward marriage, an attitude that had sorry consequences, as Eugene Kennedy shows: "The selective attention which has been given, for example, to the teachings of St. Augustine on marriage has contributed to the ecclesiastical prejudice against sexuality as a healthy element of life. Certain texts of Augustine tended to disparage sex, despite his overall praise of marriage. Sexual desire in and for itself was regarded, even in marriage, as a result of sin and as 'evil' concupiscence. Marriage, as an institution, was considered a 'remedium concupiscentiae,' a cure for concupiscence. The overtones of uneasiness about sex being barely tolerable made marriage a tenuously acceptable outlet for the emotional life of the church. This emotional coloring gave rise to the notion that marital intercourse defiled a person in some way. The use of marriage made a person unworthy to receive the Eucharist. Gradually, religion and human love became dissociated in the attitude of church teachers. As Nietzsche said, Christians for centuries begot children with a bad conscience."[15] This is a common evolution: the man who is a profligate in his youth reforms and becomes a moralist in middle age, maintaining that, even within marriage, sex and its pleasures are dangerous—a necessary evil for the begetting of children.

Gradually, the equation of sexuality with sin gained credence in the Christian world. To its credit, the official church strenuously resisted this: the Council of Trent anathematized those who held celibacy and virginity to be an inferior state to matrimony. The church itself then never considered the flesh to be intrinsically evil, but some individual churchmen certainly did, as manifested by their words and deeds. Consider four fathers of the early church. Jerome condemned the "vile body," that "sack of excrement." He was a hermit who was tormented in his cave by visions of "bevies of girls" and who grudgingly permitted marriage because it was the only way of producing virgins, the most perfect beings on earth. They were the natural "brides of Christ," he taught. Seduction of them was blasphemy, making a cuckold of Christ and, incidentally, an adulteress of the erstwhile virgin. This mania for virgins was only partially shared by his predecessor, the austere and learned Tertullian, who viewed sexual desire as the root of all evil. "The kingdom of heaven is the eunuch's fatherland." Then, without exempting virgins, he added, "Woman is the gate of hell." Another celebrated antifeminist, Clement of Alexandria, wrote, "Every woman should be overwhelmed with shame at the thought that she is a woman."[16] (The cause of women's liberation never had more ferocious opponents than these misogynistic fathers of the church.) Clement's pupil, Origen, however, was the only one of the fathers to make an issue of sexual revulsion in his own physical person. Origen castrated himself. This amputation of private parts for the sake of the heavenly kingdom was rare in Christian circles where it was officially proscribed. But it was a common practice among certain heathens: recall the earlier allusion to the fanatical priests of Cybele.

In teaching that sex, except for the procreation of children, was sinful, early and medieval churchmen created a problem. They contributed to the isolation of sexuality from love and the meaning of human relationships with disastrous results. The fanaticism of the clerical hierarchy in barely admitting sexual indulgence provoked the repressed sexual fantasies of the medieval populace to erupt in the form of defilement of the sacred. Instances of neurasthenics using a crucifix as a phallus were not unknown. (These constitute historical precedents for a similar action of the possessed girl in Peter Blatty's *The Exorcist.*) And churches became the sites of libidinous orgies. Pertinent is the chronicle of the thirteenth-century Franciscan monk, Salimbene di Adamo, written to instruct his fifteen-year-old niece in the ways of the world. He warns her of the duplicity of certain unscrupulous confessors who—in pre-confessional-box days—seduce nubile penitents behind the altar. Black Masses and incidents such as this reinforce the impression stated by James Cleugh, in *Love Locked Out,* that "the more bolts and bars the higher officers of the clergy added to the door locked against carnal love the more it insisted on flying in at the window, even the stained-glass window."[17]

Sexual delusions of grandeur among mystically inclined nuns and priests were frequent in the Middle Ages. In confession, certain nuns "related the most extraordinary hallucinations of a libidinous character. Mechthild of Magdeburg (1202–1277) felt God's hand fondling her bosom. Christine Ebner (1277–1356) believed herself with child by Jesus."[18] And according to Salimbene, there were monks who dreamed of copulating with the Virgin Mary. Cleugh indicates there were those critics of these unfortunate wearers of the coif and cowl who—acting on the assumption that the devil prompted urges below the belt—took them to be diabolically possessed, victims of "the unconquerable devil who persistently haunted these sacred precincts [convents and monasteries] in the guise of Priapus. The ancient Greek garden-god . . . with his invariable insinuating grin and erect phallus, sent a long procession of evil spirits to invade the cells. These demons took the form of either *succubi,* beautiful girls who jumped into the beds of would-be male saints, or *incubi,* handsome young men in a terrifying state of nature, who interrupted the slumbers or meditations of the

most respectable nuns."[19] The most publicized incident of
this kind occurred at an Ursuline convent in Loudun, France,
in 1634. Urban Grandier, S.J., in his capacity as chaplain, was
accused of collusion with the devil to seduce nuns, found
guilty on evidence trumped up by mass hysteria, tortured,
and executed. At the public exorcisms, staged like a circus
sideshow, the "possessed" nuns performed obscene tricks for
the spectators. At the trial, it was revealed that the repressed,
neurotic mother superior was tormented by erotic fantasies,
such as imagining herself licking the wounds of Jesus.

Throughout the Middle Ages and beyond, witches were
also believed to be in league with Satan. One proof of witchcraft was sexual congress with demons. When women accused of witchcraft were arrested, "their pubic hair was
shaved in order to make certain whether or not the devil had
branded his secret countersign on the vulva."[20] Their ensuing "confessions" are rife with references to the devil's sexual
organ. According to one deposition, "the sexual organ of the
incubus assumed a bifurcated shape at the instant of contact.
One 'prong of the pitchfork,' accordingly, penetrated the
vulva and the other the anus."[21] Another proof of witchcraft
was participation in a Black Mass. The essence of a Black
Mass is the use of a holy object or a consecrated place for
erotic satisfaction. "The maniacal fury with which the Christian rituals were befouled reached its height when a slit was
cut in the Host itself and used for producing seminal emission
in the male. In 1348 the commission of incest on the altar was
said to be the only way of avoiding, under Satan's protection,
infection by the Black Death."[22]

Perhaps no one else in medieval Christendom hammered
the sex nerve in defiance of the ecclesiastical taboo with such
monstrous perversity as the notorious satanist and sadistic
mass murderer, Gilles de Rais. A marshal of France and companion in arms to Joan of Arc, de Rais was declared at his trial
to be the chief of a coven. Soon after his exemplary association with Joan, and perhaps in despair at his inability to save
her from her harsh fate, he gradually turned to demonology.
He began by having Black Masses celebrated in his private

chapel. When this began to pall, he sought to perk up his unsurpassed appetite for desecration by coming under the tutelage of Francesco Prelati, a Florentine ex-priest, reputed to be the greatest master of abomination in the world. Prelati advised de Rais to feast exclusively on the crimes most proscribed by the church, such as raping, mutilating, and murdering kidnapped children. Over a period of eight years, de Rais tortured and ritually murdered as many as two hundred children. Shortly after he disemboweled a woman in late pregnancy to copulate with the fetus, his diet of galloping self-damnation proved too rich. He broke out in obscene hallucinations: everywhere he looked, nature tormented him with either the male organ—oblong clouds from which a flow of milky sperm drifted—or the female organ—forked boughs with a clitoral bulge. At night he suffered from lecherous dreams: succubi and incubi squeezed his genitals until he sought waking relief by prostrating himself for hours before a crucifix. His unique career in degradation was terminated by execution in 1440. The official verdict, provided by the exorcists and inquisitors, in the case of the Lord de Rais, was that he denied God through the agency of Asmodeus, the hellborn expert on erotic perversions, and that this heresy automatically turned him into a sex maniac.

The lower social classes in Western Europe in the Middle Ages were stimulated to unbridled lubricity chiefly out of ecclesiastical defiance, but the privileged classes were motivated as much by the imported tradition of pagan lasciviousness. When the Moors from North Africa conquered Spain in the eighth century, they gradually introduced into Europe a lofty ennobling concept of carnal love, refined and chivalric, and, moreover, one uninhibited by religious taboo. The Sufi mystics who accompanied the Moors, unlike their Christian counterparts who sometimes paid lip service to profane love as a bridge to the Godhead, insisted upon amorous experience as a condition necessary to the love of God. "The science of hearts" which tutored men in the amorous arts was as plainly fraught with subtlety as the contemplation of theology. Muslim sensuality, free of the misogynistic strain of the church fathers, was inseparable from Muslim mysticism. The stark contrast between the Puritanism of Christendom and the sensuality of Islam is nowhere more evident than in their polarized ideas of paradise. The Christian heaven, presided over by bodiless angels who conduct endless adoration of an all-male Trinity, appears blissfully passive and chaste. But it smacks far less of male chauvinism than the exhausting hereafter provided by Allah. Mohammedans, it would seem, pass eternity copulating. Allah's paradise is populated by innumerable virgins whose maidenheads are miraculously restored as rapidly as the faithful can perforate them. Where the pleasure instinct is so divinized, religiously imposed sexual restraint is bound to be remote, or even nonexistent. The Crusades further familiarized Western Europeans with Oriental modes of erotic enjoyment and encouraged amorous freethinking.

Much of the finest medieval literature, in rebellion against the church-mandated ideal of marital fidelity and supported by heathen enthusiasm for sexual divagations from wedlock, glorified adultery. The earliest effective glorification of adultery was organized in the twelfth century by the troubadours of Provence. They popularized the cult of romantic passion with its assertion that true love could flourish only outside marriage. The troubadours, songwriters in the guise of suppliant knights, contrived a theory of love that animated their poetry and influenced the aristocratic society for which they wrote. Love and defiance of chastity were the chief topics of their lyrics. The troubadours formulated a code, known as the doctrine of courtly love, to govern affairs of the heart between men (including clerics) and women of the highest caste. The courtly love code established the "ideal" relations that should prevail between the sexes. Courtly love taught a lover to dedicate himself wholly to the service of his lady. She must dominate; her wishes must be paramount; she must completely absorb his fidelity. He must devote his life to paying her homage in love songs and fighting in her honor. For so subjecting himself to his beloved, the lover was supposed to be purified and ennobled. The affair had to be conducted in secrecy, however, since, according to the code, marriage was not conducive to love. In practice then, the lover, displaying all the virtues save chastity, pledged his heart to a lady who was usually married to someone else. Adultery aside, the convention was idealistic, deprecating coarseness and mere sensuality.

Troubadour love affairs were regulated by what were known as "courts of love," conducted by great ladies, notably Eleanor of Aquitaine, granddaughter of the first troubadour, William of Aquitaine. The chronicler of the judgments pronounced by these courts of love, as well as the codifier of courtly love, was the worldly cleric Andreas Capellanus. His book, *The Art of Courtly Love,* evades the fact that courtly love—owing to its culmination in adultery—is irreconcilable with Christian morality, however, by postulating a higher form and a lower form. Characteristic of the higher form is his insistence on the kiss as the ultimate intimacy that the lady will grant. "And pure love is that which joins the hearts of two lovers together with a complete feeling of delight. Moreover, this love consists in the contemplation of the mind and the affection of the heart; it even goes as far as the kiss of the mouth and the embrace of the arm and the modest contact of the nude mistress except for the final solace; for those who wish to love purely are not allowed to practice that."[23] Andreas then distinguishes "pure" love from "mixed" love by saying that the latter includes "the final solace." Other devotees of *amour courtois* who had erected the system into a religion based on adultery were not pleased, needless to say, by what they considered a craven clerical concession to the church. Nonetheless, Andreas' distinction, bolstered by the practice of Platonic love, has influenced one whole school of romantic thought: sexual intercourse is not to be indulged in, for then love would die.

In any case, one feature that *amour courtois* shared with Christianity was the exaltation of womanhood. At this time, increased devotion to the Virgin Mary in Christian circles resulted in the elevation of women. Perella observes "that the cult of the Virgin and the idealization of the lady in

profane love were contemporaneous developments" reflecting "the need . . . felt in the Christian world for a female
element in the Divinity."[24] The one cult influenced the
other. Devotional hymns to the Blessed Mother influenced
the vocabulary but not the ideological sentiments of troubadour love lyrics: the flowery language of Mariolatry was converted into the flowery language of sensual love without any
supporting orthodox content. This was the case, since many
of the troubadours, as we have noted, were notorious for
their opposition to the church.

Despite the reciprocal hostility, Christianity influenced
the development of the medieval secular love lyric in other
ways also. For the devout Christian, the love of God is ecstatic by definition. The theological formulation of Christian
ecstatic love, the joyful adherence of the soul to the Beloved,
was simply transferred by the poet from God to woman. The
secularized conceit of the migration of the amorous heart is
found in the verse of the troubadours, especially in Jaufré
Rudel, who sighs, "My heart does not cease from yearning
toward her whom I love most."[25] But the conceit in the
original form, the migration of the soul to God, is never found
in the troubadours. For the two, the application to *caritas*,
as well as *cupiditas*, one must return to Augustine. After cham-
pioning the words of Ps. 73:28, "It is good for me to cling to
God," Augustine (Confessions, VI) relates his mistress' forced
separation from him: "My mistress being torn from my side
as an impediment to my marriage, my heart, which clung to
her, was racked, and wounded, and bleeding."[26] The union
of the lover and the beloved invariably, however, places God
and the lady in a position of superiority vis-à-vis the soul or
heart and the male.

Another important religious influence on the literature of
secular love was the glory-in-death theme. In the Middle
Ages, human passion was constantly borrowing sentiments
from the Passion of Christ. The motif of the profane lover
suffering cruelly on account of his lady's rejection and dying
from the "wound of love" (*vulnus amoris*) is especially significant. The *Carmina Burana,* a collection of lewd love

songs from the twelfth century, illustrates this best. Two typical lines contain the poet-lover's reference to his love wound: "Loving torments me, I die / From the wound in which I glory."[27] In a scholarly assessment of the secularization of the Christian martyrdom theme in the *Carmina Burana*, James Wilhelm concludes: "Glory in death: this is the new Christian dimension that is utterly lacking in Ovid, Catullus, and Sappho, where death is always a disaster. We must go to Prudentius' hymns to the saints or to the *Acta Martyrorum* for this tonality."[28] Ultimately, we must go to Christ, the supreme martyr for love.

Contemporaneous with the *Carmina Burana* and the secularized martyrdom theme was the romance of Tristan and Iseult and the related secularized theme of a love that leads to death. Indeed, the love story of Tristan and Iseult is the most celebrated example of the profanation of a mystic motif in the legends of medieval love. Since the adulterous lovers die simultaneously, locked in a mouth-to-mouth embrace—at least in some of the later prose versions—the fear of death, characteristic of the *Carmina Burana*, yields to the voluptuousness of death. This "dying in a swell of ecstasy," says Perella, is "the first great representation in the vernacular of the equating of death with the sexual act and vice versa."[29] Legends of medieval love that led up to the transposition of the sacred motif of a love unto death into the profane orgasm-like-death motif include the illicit adventures of Lancelot and Guinevere, Troilus and Criseyde, and Paolo and Francesca. From such celebrations of courtly love, romance shaped the great literary myths of the West and became a kind of secular religion. Christianity learned to coexist with it.

Earlier I referred to the poetry of the Sufi mystics, of whom R. A. Nicholson writes that "unless we have some clue to the writer's intention, it may not be possible to know whether his beloved is human or divine—indeed the question whether he himself always knows is one which students of Oriental mysticism cannot regard as impertinent."[30] Although this state of affairs never prevailed in the medieval literature of

Western Europe, there was a remote approximation attributable to all the borrowing. Perella formulates the crossover
this way: "The mutual influence exerted by the religious and
secular traditions of amatory literature on one another in the
Middle Ages was such that if there are no specific references
to the object of love or devotion, passages of poems and even
entire poems may be read in either key. This, of course, is
true of the Song of Songs itself, for it is a secular epi-
thalamium celebrating human love until it is subjected to an
allegorical reading in which it becomes a song of divine
love. So too the most famous medieval Latin love lyric combining Ovidian . . . and Solomonic . . . echoes is the *Iam dulcis
amica* which, perhaps with slight variants, was 'sung as a
sacred conductus at Saint-Martial or Saint-Martin in the same
decades . . . as it was performed as a sophisticated love
song.' "[31] In short, in the Middle Ages, devotional literature
idealized sex, whereas secular literature humanized religion.
Man became more like God, and God became more like
man.

    In the Renaissance period there is, again, reciprocal influ-
ence between Christian mysticism and amatory verse. But
since much of it is elaboration on duly noted medieval
themes, I shall not address myself to varying Neoplatonic
refinements. Instead, I shall allude to one highly relevant
Baroque work of art. And since the confusion between religious and sexual love within Christendom was most open in
the Middle Ages and the Renaissance-Baroque age, the latter
concentration better serves my purpose. The most justly celebrated sensuous interpretation of religious ecstasy is Bernini's famous sculpture of the transverberations of Teresa of
Ávila's heart, in the church of Santa Maria della Vittoria at
Rome. After Teresa had the ecstatic experience of encoun-
tering angelic forms who poked her dreadfully with sharp
instruments and hurt her delightfully, she vividly described
it in her autobiography, showing how the heat of divine love
burned hot in her virgin bosom. So successfully, if unintentionally, did she sensualize the spiritual that she inflamed
imaginations all over Europe; not least of all that of Bernini,

who commemorated the erotica-tinged sacred raptures in a highly stylized statue. This bravura artist depicts an ephebic seraph holding a dart and standing over a reclining Teresa, in such a way that even in the act of surrender the lavish, languorous saint appears to be the erotic aggressor. Of all Teresian art, only Richard Crashaw, in three lush devotional poems, ties the erotic knot between saint and seraph as audaciously and elegantly as Bernini.

After the Renaissance, the religio-erotic motif slumbered until the Romantic age. For Rousseau and Goethe, and a host of lesser nineteenth-century writers, lovemaking was a sacred rite. Speaking of the Romantic apotheosis of the soul-mingling kiss, in such novels as *La nouvelle Héloïse* and *The Sorrows of Young Werther,* Perella says that upon kissing the beloved, "the hero is blasted with ecstasy in a manner that recapitulates the entire amoristic tradition from the troubadours, the *dolce stil novo* poets, and Dante to Rousseau and Goethe. Paradisal nympholepsy has seldom received such glowing eloquence as . . . where the kiss of the beloved transfers all of nature into Eden regained and transforms the hero from a Saturnian into a Uranian type."[32]

Before we pass on to the modern period, which is the concern of this book, mention should be made of a long poem by Pushkin called *Gavriiliada* in which the virgin birth is eroticized. Pushkin's irresistible Mary is successively ravished by Satan, who has transformed himself from a snake to a handsome young man; by the archangel Gabriel, who bears more than the traditional celestial tidings; and finally by the Holy Spirit himself in the guise of a quivering billing dove.

The foregoing survey, brief as it is, provides historical background helpful in putting this matter in perspective. This study, let me emphasize, is not one tracing the impact of sex on modern literature or one tracing the impact of religion on modern literature—the critical woods are full of both kinds —or even a mere conjunction of the two. This is a pioneer effort working out tentative interpretations—for we are much in the realm of speculation—of what happens when these two forces are brought to bear in rich interaction upon a work of contemporary literature. Before I refine this point by a brief discussion of two novelists, let me enter a disclaimer as to comprehensiveness. Obviously, I could not refer to every writer of the twentieth century who shows religio-erotic preoccupations—even assuming I was aware of all of them. Instead, I have been forced to deal selectively with those whom I feel have displayed the concern in the most interesting and challenging way. In one or two instances this has meant including writers of relatively minor stature to the exclusion of one or two of the literary titans of our time.

The most notable omission appears to be James Joyce. It is deliberate. I struggled long with the temptation to include a chapter on Joyce before I dismissed it. My decision was motivated by the belief that while both religious and sexual strains are present in his work, only the one is there to any extent. Of his three major protagonists, Stephen, a Hamlet-like intellectual, has sublimated sex; Bloom, impotent, fetishistic, and voyeuristic, has sidestepped normal sexuality; Molly alone exhibits mature sexual interests, but even her famous monologue—and this is crucial—is entirely wanting in a sense of sin. H. G. Wells's comment on Joyce's water-closet mentality is not without merit here. For both Stephen and Bloom, the organ of reproduction is overshadowed by its function as an organ of excretion. With regard to his male characters, the stress is on micturition and even defecation. Copulation is conspicuous by its absence. The corpus of Joyce's work provides no rich interaction between sex and religion. On this score, he is concerned largely with an adolescent meld of bawdiness and blasphemy which is only tangential to the purport of this book.

However, another giant of twentieth-century literature, D. H. Lawrence, who used sex to gain entrée to the Godhead, is the foremost example of what I have in mind. He invoked the mystery of religion through orgasm. As he repeatedly pointed out, the one sure way to make sex filthy and sensual beauty degrading is to separate them from mysticism and spiritual beauty. The Lawrentian hero, the man who died, embraces the truths of the body and uses them as the basis of an unconventional but sincere religious faith. His lengthy discussions of sex veil allusions to the great religious myths of Creation, redemption, and resurrection. The Lawrentian heroine, Ursula (*The Rainbow*), in an adolescent confusion of passion with the Passion, fantasies that Christ is making love to her. The dances she dances, the songs she sings, and the music she plays are ritually erotic. Sex and religion in Lawrence's view, however, are but the media of a supreme power—nature. Through these two agencies, one can identify with animals, fish, and plants—all of whom possess sexual characteristics and achieve mystical communion. In the last analysis, Lawrence is less artist and philosopher than he is a neoreligious prophet and a neotroubadour of romance. This gives him undisputed right to the first chapter.

1

Lawrence's *The Man Who Died:*

THE HEAVENLY COCK

The Collected Letters of D. H. Lawrence (1962), edited by Harry T. Moore, is an invaluable publication for the Lawrence enthusiast, and not simply because the author clearly belongs to that small group of great letter writers. More important for the scholar, the letters make the whole line of Lawrence's life clear in a way that it had never been. This is one of the great autobiographical revelations in literary history and must have been a source of embarrassment to those pre-1962 critics who speculatively established fatuous affinities between Lawrence's life and that of his characters. The ultimate value of the letters for the researcher, at least, is that now affinities can be established without guesswork.

In a letter of February 1, 1916, D. H. Lawrence complains of Dostoevsky that he mixed "God and Sadism."[1] In an earlier letter, Lawrence asserts that love in marriage is finest "when not only the sex group of chords is attuned, but the great harmonies . . . of what we will call religious feeling" are also attuned. This statement, plus the evidence I am about to muster, entitles us to say of him that he mixed God and carnality, exhorting married couples to vibrate to the note of spiritual as well as sexual love. Lawrence broke away early from his stern Protestant upbringing, but the religious strain accompanied by "the sex melody,"[2] characteristic of all his writing, remained—notably in the letters and *The Man Who*

Died. In the latter, his last significant piece of fiction, Lawrence's innumerable allusions to Christ's passion, crucifixion, and resurrection culminate, but surprisingly it is one of the least discussed items in the Lawrence *oeuvre*. To correct this, my intention is to gloss this messianic *novella* in the light of the letters, with side-glances at two of the novels, the better to understand the Lawrentian orchestration of sex and religion. Not that the collected letters contain many direct references to *The Man Who Died:* there are but a few brief ones. However, the letters deal abundantly with related themes.

The Man Who Died is about the resurrection of Jesus according to Lawrence; more precisely, it is his reconstruction in fictive form of Christ's postresurrection life on earth, and the writing bears the stamp of sacrament. Aware of Christ as the archetypal priest of love, Lawrence, the always competitive and combative messiah *manqué*, declares in a letter written Christmas Day, 1912: "I shall always be a priest of love . . . and I'll preach my heart out."[3] Indeed, his letters are more often sermons by a man inebriated with self-brewed salvational doctrines than letters in the conventional sense.

The Man Who Died was first published in Paris in 1929 under the title of *The Escaped Cock*, a perfect title, given the demons Lawrence wrestled with. But, probably at the insistence of his British publisher, the author changed to the present title shortly before his death in 1930. He summarized the story and explained the inception as follows: "I wrote a story of the Resurrection, where Jesus gets up and feels very sick about everything, and can't stand the old crowd any more—so cuts out—and as he heals up, he begins to find what an astonishing place the phenomenal world is, far more marvellous than any salvation or heaven—and thanks his stars he needn't have a 'mission' any more. It's called *The Escaped Cock*, from that toy in Volterra." His correspondent, Earl Brewster—according to Moore's note beneath the letter—"recalled that they were in Grosseton [not Volterra] on Easter morning, where they 'passed a little shop, in the window of which was a toy white rooster escaping from an egg. I remarked that it suggested a title—*The*

Escaped Cock—A Story of the Resurrection.' "[4] Lawrence's
literary agent, Laurence Pollinger, having expressed some
concern for the possible blasphemous character of the story,
is reassured by Lawrence, who also, incidentally, passes a
value judgment on his own work. "It's one of my best stories.
And Church doctrine teaches the resurrection of the body;
and if that doesn't mean the whole man, what does it mean?
And if man is whole without a woman then I'm damned. No,
you are wrong."

This remark contains in essence the criticism directed at
Christ by a man whose genius, his "demon" he called it, is
more religious in character than concerned with politics and
social issues. A religious, if often heretical, aura surrounds his
best writings. This is especially true of *The Man Who Died,*
where he faults Christ for two reasons, principally. He bun-
gled the resurrection, permitting himself to be "overcome
by the shadow of death." And by persisting in celibacy, after
his restoration to life and before his ascension, he par-
ticipated in "a useless afterdeath."[5] The following passage
from *The Rainbow* (1915) amounts to a preview of *The Man
Who Died:* "The Resurrection is to life, not to death. Shall I
not see those who have risen again walk here among men
perfect in body and spirit, whole and glad in the flesh, living
in the flesh, loving in the flesh, begetting children in the flesh,
arrived at last to wholeness, perfect without scar or blemish,
healthy without fear of ill-health? Is this not the period of
manhood and of joy and fulfillment, after the Resurrection?"[6] Lawrence's concept of resurrection is humanistic and
naturalistically utopian, not eschatological and transcenden-
tally teleological. That Christ should have been resurrected
with the gaping wound in his side, into which doubting
Thomas was invited to thrust his finger, was abhorrent to
Lawrence.

The man who died is supposed to be Christ, although,
throughout the narrative, he is simply called "the man who
had died." Actually he stands for the author, Lawrence himself "writ large." Christ was Lawrence's favorite impersona-
tion. But he did not think of Christ as God. Christ was, in-

stead, the greatest of human beings. "Christ was infinitely good," he says, in a letter of April 9, 1911, "but mortal as we."[7] William Troy is surely right when he argues that long before *The Man Who Died,* throughout much of his life, in fact, Lawrence identified himself with Christ in "the persecutions and humiliations, the journeys by water, the agonies in the wilderness, the betrayals and final apotheosis at the hands of his disciples."[8] When we add resurrections and sermons on the mount to this list, we perceive clearly the degree to which Lawrence interposed himself between the historical person and the fictional model.

The man who died bears little resemblance to the Christ of the Gospels, once the latter is filtered through Lawrence. To begin with, the crucifixion was not fatal, and the man who died rises from the tomb ultimately for the sake of the body and to promote a vision of the meaning of sexuality for salvation. As he explains to the first person he meets after he leaves the crypt: "Don't be afraid. . . . I am not dead. They took me down too soon."[9] He swooned on the cross, survives his crucifixion, and recovers in the tomb. He escapes "without desire, without even the desire to live, empty save for the all-overwhelming disillusion that lay like nausea where his life had been. Yet perhaps, deeper even than disillusion, was a desireless resoluteness."[10] But gradually he is roused from this torpid stupor by a young gamecock and by the example of nature in the advancing springtime. "The man who had died stood and watched the cock who had escaped and been caught, ruffling himself up, rising forward on his toes, throwing up his head, and parting his beak in another challenge from life to death. The brave sounds rang out, and though they were diminished by the cord round the bird's leg, they were not cut off. The man who had died looked nakedly on life, and saw a vast resoluteness everywhere flinging itself up in stormy or subtle wave-crests, foam-tips emerging out of the blue invisible, a black and orange cock or the green flame-tongues out of the extremes of the fig tree. They came forth, these things and creatures of spring, glowing with desire and with assertion. They came like crests of foam, out of the blue flood of the invisible desire, out of the vast invisible sea of strength, and they came coloured and tangible, evanescent, yet deathless in their coming."[11]

The man who died, like Lawrence himself, takes heart from the very nature that he admires: for no animal, however frustrated, is separated from self in desireless fashion; and buds, moving out from the stem, flower thoughtlessly, according to harmonious laws. This "determined surge of life" provokes him to reassess his mission, and he concludes that he has outlived it. "I was wrong to try to interfere" in the souls of men, to offer "unphysical" salvation. His public life is over: the teacher and the savior are dead in him. As he explains to Madeleine, an unsympathetically presented Mary Magdalene, both of them ran to excess. "You," he tells her, "took more than you gave," from your lovers in the past. Whereas "I, in my mission . . . gave more than I took."[12] Madeleine destroyed her adorers; he was destroyed by his adorers. His private life commences with a vow to seek balance, to avoid the folly, in his case, of giving without taking. As if to prove it, he solicits gold pieces from the reformed prostitute.

At this point in the story, Lawrence is evidently criticizing the self-renunciatory character of Christ. He accuses him of having loved imperfectly. For the essence of love, as Lawrence experienced it, is summed up in a statement from a letter of August 19, 1912. "At any rate, and whatever happens, I do love, and I am loved. I have given and I have taken —and that is eternal."[13] He relates Christ's practice of turning the other cheek to incomplete loving. In a letter of July 16, 1916, he says, "The great Christian tenet must be surpassed, there must be something new": no more "turning the other cheek." Based on reaction and negation, embodying only half the eternal truth, it is the way of death. "What we want is the fulfillment of our desires, down to the deepest and most spiritual desire."[14]

Christ's failure, in Lawrence's view, was ultimately a failure in self-fulfillment. Other historical figures reviled by Lawrence for the same fault are Dostoevsky, Van Gogh, and

E. M. Forster. Since he sees them all as belonging to the same anti-natural, life-hating tradition, their shortcomings are Christ's. The novels of Dostoevsky are denounced in a letter to Middleton Murry and Katherine Mansfield. "They are great parables . . . but false art," since he used all his characters "as theological or religious units." Dostoevsky was both obsessed by Christ and terrified of him; as a result, his characters illustrate this split. Alyosha Karamazov and Prince Myshkin represent their creator's "desire for the spiritual, turn-the-other-cheek consummation"; Dmitri Karamazov and Rogozhin the equally urgent "desire to achieve the sensual, all-devouring consummation." Christian ecstasy, when it is accompanied by the desire to be "devoured in the body,"[15] leads to idiocy. Sensual ecstasy, when it is accompanied by guilt, leads to murder.

Van Gogh is another who could not "set the angel of himself clear in relation to the animal of himself." Had he been able truly to relate the two, "he need not have cut off his ear and gone mad," says a letter of March 1, 1915. In the face of the universal "yearning to procreate oneself," the artist has four alternatives. He may submit fearfully, like most artists, to his uneasy animal self and watch *"his art . . . come out of that"* with difficulty. He may resist, "like Fra Angelico." Like Van Gogh, he may choose the worst alternative: offer no resistance, nor submission, and in that event go mad. Or "best of all . . . live one's animal" creatively, *"be the artist creating a man in living fact* (not like Christ, as Van Gogh wrongly said)." Then the art would be "the final expression of the created animal or man,"[16] not the artist's justification as in the first alternative.

No more than the others did E. M. Forster, Lawrence's occasional houseguest, find the solution and become "pregnant with his own soul." In a lengthy letter to Bertrand Russell, Lawrence describes Forster as "a resigned soul. But a resigned soul is not a free soul. A resigned soul has yielded its claim on temporal living. It can only do this because the temporal living is being done for it vicariously. Therefore it is dependent on the vicar, let it say what it will. So Christ, who resigned his life, only resigned it because he knew the others would keep theirs. They would do the living, and would later adapt his method to their living. The freedom of the soul within the denied body is a sheer conceit." Forster yielded his "claim on temporal living" by denying his body "the freedom of the soul" that comes from going to a woman. "His ultimate desire . . . the desire to work for humanity . . . is every man's ultimate desire and need." But this requires self-discovery and a satisfied manhood. "Immediate physical action,"[17] not poetry, is the answer. If Forster had dared to go to a woman, he would have received the knowledge— of himself, of herself, and beyond these of the unknown— necessary to act for humanity.

Few men have ever expected so much from intimacy with a woman and made such enormous claims for intimacy as Lawrence. Over and over again, the letters tell us why he turns to a woman and the revelation he receives: to be "re-born, re-constructed . . . to get one's soul and body satisfied . . . so that one is free from oneself"[18]; to "fertilise the soul . . . to vision or being"[19]; to gain "great blind knowledge and suffering and joy. . . . Because the source of all life and knowledge is in man and woman, and the source of all living is in the interchange and the meeting and mingling of these two."[20] In this exalted view, of course, "love is a much bigger thing than passion, and a woman *much* more than sex."[21] He provides a vision of the meaning of woman for salvation.

This brings us to the core of Lawrence's quarrel with Jesus. The knowledge of a woman is indispensable if any man would act to better humanity, but Jesus knew not a woman. He tried to sustain spiritual love without sensual love. "Christ was profoundly, disastrously wrong," says a letter of January 26, 1925. He sought for wholeness in celibacy, "that unreal half thing." He was wanting in that "warm flame of life [which] is worth all the spiritualness and delicacy and Christlikeness on this miserable globe."[22] Moreover, since the ultimate beauty resides in the revelations established through

contact between the female body and the male body, sexual
fulfillment is more religious than sexual denial. In *The Rainbow,* Lawrence voluptuously develops the cult of bodily mysticism: the realization of supreme "Absolute Beauty, in the
body of woman."[23] Holding asceticism against Christianity,
he occupies common ground with the Yeats of "Among
School Children," who also finds bruising the body to please
the soul a sinister act. Heroically Lawrence struggled against
his Puritan heritage: against the notion that the sexual act is
lustful, immoral, and death-producing. Ostensibly he is trying to convince the reader that it is fatal to separate love and
sexuality; actually, he is trying to persuade himself.

When the man who died first appears, he is on the margin
of life, in a touch-me-not stage of resurrection. Here he
resembles the risen Jesus who cautioned his mother: "Touch
me not; for I am not yet ascended to my Father" (John 20:17).
But the resemblance is short-lived; Lawrence, as was his bent
—exploring characters through their sexual natures—soon
furnishes carnal excitation, supplying the man who died with
a "warm flame."[24] At the farmhouse where he recovers, he
is roused by the peasant's seductive wife. Even though he
does not touch her, for she is possessive—a trait she shares
with Madeleine—the incident is revelatory, opening up new
vistas. He no longer sees himself as the most exalted sacrificial savior, but as the castrate par excellence, the lowly dupe
of holy women, greedy in their virtue. These women, who
surrounded him during his ministry, adored the epicene ascetic in him to the chagrin of the man in him, so that he
resolves to serve them no more. He resigns as the Son of
Woman. Lawrence is relieved. In a letter to Middleton
Murry, he prophesies: "I'm afraid there'll be no more Son
Saviours. One was almost too much, in my opinion."[25] Male
strength, manifesting itself in heroic deeds, is what Lawrence admires. In a letter to his mother-in-law, he confides:
"A man must be more than nice and good . . . heroes are
worth more than saints. . . . I am no Jesus that lies on his
mother's lap."[26]

Lawrence was more sympathetic to the historical Mary

Magdalene than to Madeleine, her fictional counterpart. Two letters, written prior to the composition of *The Man Who Died*, leave the impression that when he comes to write his version of the life of Christ he will depict them as lovers. The first, November 7, 1917, suggests that Christ was inhibited by fear from recognizing her as the true agent of his salvation. "If Jesus had paid more attention to Magdalene, and less to his disciples, it would have been better. . . . The pure understanding between the Magdalene and Jesus went deeper than the understanding between the disciples and Jesus."[27] The second, May 28, 1927, is projected wish fulfillment. "I finished my 'Resurrection' picture, and like it. It's Jesus stepping up, rather grey in the face, from the tomb, with his old ma helping him from behind, and Mary Magdalene easing him up towards her bosom in front."[28] Why then does Lawrence have the man who died reject Madeleine? To write the novelette, he had to ponder the Christ-Magdalene relationship as never before, and so I conjecture that the special character of her acquired virtue occurred to him for the first time. The typical prostitute despises the flesh while she plys her trade, and even if she reforms, she continues to despise it. But Lawrence insists that Madeleine the prostitute heartily enjoyed sex, whereas Madeleine the saint loathes what she used to enjoy most. Reverence for the body, instead of revulsion, is the natural virtue a woman must possess if she is to appeal properly to a man whose problem is latent virility.

The man who died intuitively understands this, and so he turns away from a prostitute emeritus, whose "love had passed," and a mean-souled peasant woman, whose love had not yet begun, to find his regeneration as a man in the arms of a healing priestess, whose love is in full flood. Her acceptance of him is free of the fret and compulsion he has known with Madeleine. She offers him the "courage of life," not the "courage of death"; the touch of her love, not "the corpse of her love." And "suddenly it dawned on him: I asked them all to serve me with the corpse of their love. And in the end I offered them only the corpse of my love. This is my body—

take and eat."[29] In shame, he repudiates bodiless love and mounts a phallic resurrection with the priestess, heralded by the cry, "I am risen." When the contact is consummated, and "the man and the woman were fulfilled of one another,"[30] he is reborn. The man who died is finally filled to the brim with a love of life through a life of love, in the sense of amatory tenderness.

The Man Who Died also illustrates Lawrence's central doctrine, nowhere else so succinctly expressed as in a letter of January 17, 1913: "My great religion is a belief in the blood, the flesh, as being wiser than the intellect. We can go wrong in our minds. But what our blood feels and believes and says, is always true."[31] This biological worship is complete with icons, as attested to by a letter of February 27, 1927: "the phallus is a great sacred image."[32] And Lawrence, full of "phallic glow,"[33] is the prophet of "phallic consciousness, which . . . is not the cerebral sex-consciousness, but something really deeper, and the root of poetry."[34] His private phallic religion is opposed to Christianity but in harmony with certain ancient fertility cults. He chides cerebralized Christianity for failing to teach us "that after our Crucifixion, and the darkness of the tomb, we shall rise again in the flesh."[35] But the old, dark religions understood the tragedy of sex-in-the-head, instead of down where it belongs. " 'God enters from below,' said the Egyptians, and that's right. Why can't you darken your minds, and know that the great gods pulse in the dark, and enter you as darkness through the lower gates. Not through the head. Why don't you seek again the unknown and invisible gods who step sometimes into your arteries, and down the blood vessels to the phallus, to the vagina, and have strange meetings there?"[36] Lawrence's life moved on a dark tide of blood. By combining primitive creeds with the new psychology, he conceives what amounts to a quasi-physiological religion in which the gods are darkness, the church is the body, and the sacrament is sex.

Lawrence is like some Old Testament prophet, fulminating against the sins of his contemporaries. He is even a prophet in another sense. Long before the slogan "Black is beautiful" became fashionable, he celebrated the rites of the dark gods in exotic, usually primitive settings—Mexico, New Mexico, or Australia. But he is a prophet without honor. During his lifetime, he was subject to police harassment: the British authorities seized his paintings and suppressed his writings. He was branded a pornographer and hounded by censor-morons. They were profoundly wrong; he is the opposite of a pornographer. Where the pornographer depersonalizes sex, depicts the body as inconcinnous and polluted, and panders to the basest urges; Lawrence subdues his art to an erotic metaphysics, depicts the body as beautiful and good, and labors "to make the sex relation valid and precious, instead of shameful."[37] Promiscuous sex and copulation for male masturbation are the pornographer's stock-in-trade. But one of Lawrence's most important declarations of the amatory reality is: "Nothing nauseates me more than promiscuous sex."[38] The anointed phallus and the god-congested vagina are too holy to be abused. As to the man who uses a woman to masturbate himself, Lawrence's scorn is great: "he is *merely* repeating a known reaction upon himself, not seeking a new reaction, a discovery." Sex-contact with another individual should always bring a "new connection or progression,"[39] and should be characterized by "a sense of renewal and deeper being afterwards."[40] And certainly the long quotation near the end of the paragraph directly preceding indicates that Lawrence's theatrical view of the sexual parts as paradisic is at odds with the pornographer's tormented view of them as hellish.

Lawrence's rejection of pornography is total; his repudiation of Christianity only partial. Toward the latter, he engages in a love-hate ambivalence. After all, he writes: "I realize that the greatest thing the world has seen is Christianity, and one must be endlessly thankful for it." In the same letter, however, he adds this qualification: "But I count Christianity as one of the great historical factors, the has-been. That is why . . . I am not a Christian."[41] He considers Christianity a "has-been" for a number of reasons, several of which have been alluded to already. Christianity is anti life in a twofold way. First, it extols living for an afterlife rather than for this life. Further, it is responsible for the repression of true sexuality and a sublimation, in a ritualistic way, of sexual impulse. Again Christianity is too cerebral: it is responsible for inhibiting the forces of instinct. As an agency of repression and inhibition, it prevents man from becoming a three-dimensional object: moving and attaining equilibrium among plants and animals and relating himself to them with forces of life deeper than intelligence. Lawrence's rage is ultimately directed at Christian theology. He denies the concept of God as primarily a transcendent being, viewing him instead as immanent in sensory reality where he can be encountered pantheistically. While the traditional theologian worships the Creator, Lawrence worships creation.

He was not a Christian for certain other reasons that remain to be touched upon. To begin with, he has no sympathy with martyrdom of any kind. "I hate those who seek martyrdom. One wants victory."[42] Even the crucifixion of Jesus is no exception. "Jesus becomes more *unsympatisch* to me, the longer I live: crosses and nails and tears and all that stuff."[43] The Christian presupposition that martyrdom can lead to victory—and under some circumstances might be the only way to triumph—he disallows. He is adamant on the point: he further disallows the modern Christian distinction between desirable, freely chosen martyrdom, the crucifixion, and undesirable, involuntary martyrdom, *autos da fe.* And to reinforce it, he interpolates Asiatic and pagan allusions. "No more crucifixions, no more martyrdoms, no more *autos da fe.* . . . Every crucifixion starts a most deadly chain of Karma, every martyr is a Laocoön snake to tangle up the human family."[44]

Lawrence's initial objection to the "crosses and nails" of Jesus is the standard Freudian interpretation: the cross is a castration symbol. He first expresses this misgiving in *The Rainbow.* "In religion there were the two great motives of fear and love. The motive of fear was as great as the motive of love. Christianity accepted crucifixion to escape from fear; 'Do your worst to me, that I may have no more fear of the worst.' "[45] The craven motive of fear that he here imputes to Christianity is supported by an aforementioned incident in *The Man Who Died*. When the female followers of the man who died piously grovel at his feet, they are wielding worship as a weapon of castration. To escape an unpleasant, more and more inevitable fate imposed by others, he chooses a measure of self-determination, in panic, while there is still time. Before they can destroy him, he will accept crucifixion and destroy himself.

Lawrence's second objection to the Good Friday spectacle is curious, given the traditional notion that the death of Jesus was and is unparalleled in the annals of self-sacrifice. His dissent is way-out: he charges Christ with egoism. "The Egoist as a divine figure on the Cross, held up to tears and love and veneration, is to me a bit nauseating."[46] The crucifixion is traditionally exalted as the perfect example in all history of the commandment, "Love thy neighbor as thyself" (Mark 12:31). Again Lawrence demurs, and the following explains the basis of his disagreement: "Is there nothing beyond my fellow man? If not, then there is nothing beyond myself, beyond my own throat, which may be cut, and my own purse, which may be slit: because *I* am the fellow-man of all the world, my neighbour is but myself in a mirror. So we toil in a circle of pure egoism. This is what 'love thy neighbour as thyself' comes to." This position, that "Christianity is based on the love of self, the love of property, one degree removed,"[47] if not true in theory has, unfortunately, all too often been true in practice. But the implication, contained in an earlier letter, that Christ should have atoned for egoism rather than sin is hard to understand in view of the fact that the former, under the name of pride, is one of the seven deadly sins.

Lawrence's further condemnation of this commandment on another count—"This is what the love of our neighbour has brought us to, that, because one man dies, we all die"—is more to the point, however. The inference here is that much of Christianity, a little in love with death, mistakenly insists that suffering and victimhood were the whole of

Christ's life—the good news he wanted to bring us. Something in the Christian tradition was allowed to become grotesque in its glorification of suffering for its own sake. Too many Christians have used suffering as a neurotic escape from the far more demanding task of self-fulfillment. Lawrence shows profound insight into this needlessly debilitating preoccupation with pain, self-affliction, and guilt in an apothegm on soldiers motivated by the Christian ideal. "They are all so brave, to suffer, but none of them brave enough, to reject suffering."[48]

This rejection of suffering where the pursuit of property and power is concerned is not to be construed, however, as a blanket repudiation of the efficacy of human suffering. Lawrence examines the place of pain in our lives as it relates to love and heartily approves. "One must learn to love, and go through a good deal of suffering to get to it, like any knight of the grail, and the journey is always *towards* the other soul, not away from it. Do you think love is an accomplished thing, the day it is recognised? It isn't. To love, you have to learn to understand the other, more than she understands herself, and to submit to her understanding of you. It is damnably difficult and painful, but it is the only thing which endures." Lawrence calls this "my message as far as I've got any."[49] Since he considers suffering an inescapable means to self-perfection and hallows it by the use of "the grail" simile, the careless charge brought against him by pietistic contemporaries, that he was an irreligious hedonist, is utterly without foundation.

Breeding death and egoism, the great commandment, in Lawrence's view, is unfortunate in another respect also. " 'Love thy neighbour as thyself'—well and good, if you'll hate thy neighbour as thyself."[50] This recalls one of Bernard Shaw's most celebrated epigrams: "Do not love your neighbor as yourself. If you are on good terms with yourself it is an impertinence: if on bad, an injury."[51] Let both the self-adorer and the self-abhorrer take heed.

Another bar to Lawrence's acceptance of Christianity is his relationship with his wife, Frieda Weekley. During their courtship, complicated by the fact that she is already another man's wife, Lawrence sees this woman—six years his senior, by the way—as a female divinity. He woos her with such words as: "I am in your hands—'into thine hand, O Lord, I commend,' etc. I want you to do as you like ... your will is my will."[52] Throughout the love letters, this private goddess receives homage. She inspires awe in him and makes him feel like a monk. He is going to her "to start living" and "to be born" anew. This acolyte, about to marry a religion, has little need for Christianity; it could only provide rivalry. Their impending marriage would be a eucharistic experience. Frieda's role, he implies, is to be that of a wet nurse. "You make me think of Maupassant's story. An Italian workman, a young man, was crossing in the train to France, and had no money, and had eaten nothing for a long time. There came a woman with breasts full of milk—she was going into France as a wet nurse. Her breasts full of milk hurt her—the young man was in a bad way with hunger. They relieved each other and went their several ways."[53] But Frieda is not always the martyrologist of sexual experience; sometimes Lawrence would be the consumed host. For as he tells Katherine Mansfield: "In a way, Frieda is the devouring mother."[54] As pronounced as the oral character of this relationship is the son-lover aspect, which I shall develop subsequently. Common to both, however, is a continual struggle for dominance, a prolonged love battle, with one sex partner trying to subjugate and degrade the other.

On the manifest level, *The Man Who Died* is the greatest story ever told as "translated" by D. H. Lawrence. On the latent or autobiographical level, it is both the mythical formulation and the idealized presentation of his unsatisfactory marriage. Lawrence mythologizes himself into the man who died and Frieda into the priestess of Isis. The priestess serves the goddess who awaits the fecundation of her womb by Osiris, the once mutilated god, now risen. Goddess surrogate, the priestess patiently saves her virginity for him who is reborn. The recurrent metaphor is that of the lotus bud waiting for the right kind of sun: not "the golden brief day-suns

of show" nor "the hard winter suns of power" but "the pene-
tration of the flooding, violet-dark sun that has died and risen
and makes no show."[55] At sunset, one day, an unprepossess-
ing stranger seeking shelter approaches the temple. The
priestess puts him up in a cave where the water supply issues
from a rock fringed with "maidenhair fern," and the dietary
staple is bread and wine. When she beholds his scarred hands
and feet, she is touched, for the first time, "with the flame-tip
of life."[56] And when he joins her in ritual at the temple, it
occurs to her that Isis has brought this vagabond "home to
herself." The priestess detains him, certain that he is the lost
Osiris. The stranger responds in kind; he too feels the shock
of love coupled to desire, for the first time. In the consummation that ensues before the shrine, the Lady of Isis heals the
man who died: "the death aloofness"[57] is dissolved, and he is
absorbed into greater life than he has ever known before.

On the surface, *The Man Who Died* chronicles the transformation of the celibate man who died into the phallic Osiris, under the protection of the sun. And here, of course,
there is no reference to Lawrence's marriage. But on a sub-
surface, Lawrence is rewriting his forlorn premarital and
marital history. The cave is a case in point. Apart from its
suitability for the man who died—since his spiritual resurrection takes place in one cave, it is fitting that his physical
resurrection should be prepared for in another—the womb-
like cave, on the autobiographical plane, betrays Lawrence's
excessive maternal solicitude, the backwash of his Oedipal
fixation. He freely admits the dilemma that it poses for his
love life, one that he dramatizes brilliantly and at length in
Sons and Lovers (1913). Lawrence, the self-proclaimed "son-
lover"—in an unpublished foreword to *Sons and Lovers*—
laments what happens when a "son-lover takes a wife . . . she
is not his wife, she is only his bed." He desperately wants
Frieda to be something more than a "bed," but the inexora-
ble deadweight of the past keeps dragging him back to the
"cave." This counterpull accounts for his vacillatory behavior
during courtship. So often, despite his torrid love letters,
when Frieda would press for an assignation, he would stall,

with such remarks as "Look, my dear, . . . we can wait ever a bit religiously for one another."[58]

His emotional development stunted by his mother's possessive love, Lawrence could not give himself to any woman with carefree abandon. His compensation is twofold. If he could not have all the physical fulfillment he desired, he would have spiritual plenty. That is why the religious dimension is so frequently an intruder in matters of the heart, even when least expected as in the previous quotation. It hardly seems an apt comment from a man who professed to despise asceticism. Also, if life forced him to accept the role of passive victim of maternal power, he would use fiction to get even: wish-fulfillment stories in which he is the ultimate victor. *Sons and Lovers* is the most direct reversal of the drift toward extinction—for in the closing lines of the novel, Paul, a portrait of Lawrence as a young man, is made, most unconvincingly, to turn from death toward life—but *The Man Who Died* is the most subliminal. The woman of Isis taking death out of the man who died is, on a latent level, Frieda performing a similar task for Lawrence. Powerless to put into the real world the power he knows he has within, this overwomaned man instead works his will with words in a desperate daydream.

The cave only symbolizes the womb, both the real smothering maternal womb and the fancied liberating wifely womb. The cave literally contains "a little basin of rock where the maidenhair fern fringed a dripping mouthful of water."[59] In fantasies and dreams, where free association is the key to understanding, "maidenhair" would appear to be shorthand for maidenhead and the pubic hair of a virgin. "Fern" following "maidenhair" probably represents in microcosm all the flora on the temple grounds, which is in natural sympathy with the virgin priestess. And recalling the earlier metaphor of a lotus bud waiting for a certain sun, there lurks the promise of flowering maidenhood. These connotations, in turn, reflect Lawrence's own paradoxical interest in virginity. Despite the judgment of the man who died, "virginity is a form of greed,"[60] Lawrence, in reality, associ-

ates the condition with women he loves. He and his mother
enacted a virgin-child, if not a Virgin-Christ, tableau, never
acknowledging the fatherhood of the man in the family. The
virgin-mother coexists with the son-lover, satisfying the unconscious impulses of both. It enables the woman to replace
her despised husband, at least Platonically, with a taboo
libidinal partner, while it enables the young man to replace
his despised father on the same terms. The temptation to
repeat the triangular game with Frieda, an older woman also
married to an offensive man, must have been strong.

The water and rock images are also significant. When the
man who died satisfies his hunger by washing wine-soaked
bread down with water, the gesture portends the eucharistic
character of his forthcoming nuptials. And so art improves
upon life. Lawrence's most idealized self, the man who died,
unlike Lawrence for whom the nursing situation was the
paradisal one, is able to achieve the putative goal: investing
orgasm with the quality of sacrament. And thus the priestess,
unlike Frieda the nursing-mother proxy, is free to be dear to
her man, as he puts it, "in the middle of my being."[61] In *The
Man Who Died*, the infantile-nursing fantasy is transformed
into mature, if romantically glorified, coitus, and the hoped-
for holy communion in marriage is approximated. Apart
from autobiographical implications, the man who died is
twice entombed in a rocky cavern, and a stone in the latter
one is associated with life-giving water. The first cavern is a
tomb, a religious vault for a redeemer; the second cavern is
the objective correlative of the vagina of the priestess, a
mother-earth figure. The first recalls the rock upon which
Peter was presented with the keys to the kingdom; the second is the Lawrentian response to T. S. Eliot's "dry stone"
where there is "no sound of water."

Frieda begot three children by her first husband, Ernest
Weekley, a professor of languages, before she abandoned
him and eloped with Lawrence in 1912. Since Weekley had
once been Lawrence's teacher, he was something of a father
figure to the younger man. The Oedipal ravages are rampant
here. By bedding the mother and mocking the father in front

of the children, Lawrence "slays" Weekley and more: he vicariously dishonors his own deceased father. Even in death the Oedipal man cannot let go. And this incident from life is related, in *The Man Who Died*, to the most grandiose wish fulfillment imaginable—deicide. After the risen man has repudiated the remainder of his messianic mission, he mocks the prophesied ascension. Observing "the flame of life" in the peasant's tethered cock, he says: "Surely thou art risen to the Father, among birds."[62] And on the road to Emmaus, he baits two disciples, to whom he has not disclosed himself, asking them how it shall be fulfilled.

> "Then how will he [the Master] ascend?"
> "As Elijah the Prophet, he shall go up in a glory."
> "Even into the sky."
> "Into the sky."
> "Then he is not risen in the flesh?"
> "He is risen in the flesh."
> "And will he take flesh up into the sky?"
> "The Father in Heaven will take him up."[63]

It is surprising that Lawrence did not see how, in this messianic fantasy, the cherished will to love is succeeded by the contemptible will to power precisely when the Son chooses to defy and travesty the Father's will.

No more than the man who died can Lawrence "ascend unto the Father." The act of writing is, for Lawrence, a ritual Oedipal act. His stories are strewed with paternal corpses and virgin mothers. In *The Rainbow*, for example, Anna Brangwen seeks to deny, by ritualized dancing, her impregnation by her husband. "She took off her things and danced. . . . She would dance his nullification, she would dance to her unseen Lord. She was exalted over him, before the Lord. . . . And she lifted her hands and danced again, to annul him . . . dancing his non-existence. . . . He watched, and his soul burned in him. He turned aside, he could not look, it hurt his eyes. Her fine limbs lifted and lifted, her hair was sticking out all fierce, and her belly, big, strange, terrifying, uplifted to the Lord. Her face was rapt and beautiful, she danced exulting before her Lord, and knew no man."[64] Not only does she have a virgin complex, but she fancies herself the Virgin Mary. On another occasion during her first pregnancy, Anna castrates her husband in a more exalted way. Instead of seeking his nullification, she just deprives him of his body: she confuses him with the archangel Gabriel. "Sometimes, when he stood in the doorway, his face lit up, he seemed like an Annunciation to her. . . . And she watched him, suspended. He had a dark, burning being that she dreaded and resisted. She was subject to him as to the Angel of the Presence."[65]

Unconsciously, Lawrence writes continually to murder his hated father anew. But if his revenge on the father—whose crime is to have sexual relations with the mother Lawrence covets and who perforce he must turn into a virgin to diminish the dreaded fear of incest, a fear, according to Jung, of being devoured by the mother—is petty in *The Rainbow,* it takes on cosmic dimensions in *The Man Who Died.* By shooting down God the Father, bringing low the supreme father figure in the universe, and by mating with a virgin goddess and impregnating her, Lawrence exceeds the Oedipal man's wildest dreams. No wonder he was so fond of his achievement in *The Man Who Died,* even though it does not at all illustrate his dictum that he used his art for self-catharsis, to shed his sickness—"art for my sake." The opposite is true. Far from healing him, his fictions are frequently grandiose masturbatory exercises, all marinated in religion, masochism, and narcissism.

All too often, in practice, his art was used to stoke his quasi-paranoidal delusions: to advertise the public Lawrence who recklessly poured kerosine on the flame of life; and to conceal the private Lawrence who knew his life and loves to be passive and even unmanly. Behind the gap between art and life, the public image and the private reality, is the matter of rapport. William Gass expresses it pithily. "Lawrence among the flowers and the animals: how free he felt, how accepted, how alive—until he returned to Frieda who stood in the doorway, absorbing the light." Gass explains the breakdown in human rapport as owing to Lawrence's complex personality and the reaction of others to it. "Lawrence was right, there was a lover living in him, a great one, an *über-mensch*, a celebrator of life, a healthy soul; but there was also Lawrence the weasel, the little frightened momma-boy, the death-seeker, the denier, the sick and terribly weak one, opening his coat to flourish before us a phallus in the form of a flower." Lawrence was torn asunder between life-affirming and life-denying impulses. He was a genius and a prophet, but this did not save him from "a life lived at low wick."[66] When the human world attacks him and reminds him of his inability to live up to his enormous potential, he strikes back. He feels himself to be a rejected genius, a ridiculed prophet, and so for the pain inflicted on him, he inflicts pain on others. To the dying Katherine Mansfield, he sends a venomous letter written to himself: "I loathe you. You revolt me stewing in your consumption. . . . The Italians were quite right to have nothing to do with you."[67]

However, though his writings failed to restore him to health, they gloriously transmuted neurosis into art. His awe-inspiring sensuous concreteness, his visual-poetic talent; his responsiveness to emotional states, sensory experience, and nature hinged to his overall creative genius produced unsurpassed studies of sexual and psychological relations between men and women. The literature Lawrence created is centered around the difficulties of loving and the pressures that both self and society interpose between individuals and their fulfillment in a dehumanizing modern world. It has universal appeal.

The pursuit of religious ideals divorced from sexual fulfillment is self-destructive. That is an important legacy left by Lawrence. One of his foremost heirs in this bequest is William Golding. How Golding spends his patrimony is the subject of the next chapter.

2

Golding's *The Spire:*

THE PRAYER AND THE PHALLUS

1

Sexuality is treated with greater religious gravity in William Golding's *The Spire* than in probably any other contemporary novel. *The Spire* is a symbolic novel told entirely from the point of view of Jocelin, the fourteenth-century dean of a thirteenth-century English cathedral, who is obsessed with the belief that it is his divine mission to add a four-hundred-foot spire to the Cathedral Church of Our Lady. "God revealed it to me in a vision." He prevails over the combined opposition of clergy and builders who rightfully suspect that the cathedral rests on a mud foundation. Dean Jocelin displays a proprietary interest in the cathedral: it is his Bible in stone, and the spire is to be his prayer rising from it. But the spire has a will of its own: it is a compelling symbolic presence, having twin significance as a gigantic phallus in stone as well as a prayer in stone, "a diagram of the highest prayer of all."[1]

The phallic symbolism is established in the microcosmic description of the cathedral model: "The model was like a man lying on his back. The nave was his legs placed together, the transepts on either side were his arms outspread. The choir was his body; and the Lady Chapel, where now the services would be held, was his head. And now also, springing, projecting, bursting, erupting from the heart of the building, there was its crown and majesty, the new spire."[2] What is obvious from the beginning to the reader brought up in a Freudian ambience, the phallus of a supine man, is absent from the dean's conscious mind at the outset. Only as he gradually and painfully discovers his repressed sexuality does it dawn on him what his expressed godliness has concealed.

The novel opens with the earliest stage of construction and closes with the spire completed and Jocelin dead. But the development of the novel should be traced through Jocelin's growing awareness of his repressed manliness. In preconstruction days, years before the tale begins, we are told that, in what appeared to him to be an unselfish desire to secure the happiness of another, he arranged a marriage for Pangall, the crippled cathedral caretaker—whose impotence Jocelin refused to recognize at the time—with Goody, a sexually appealing girl. For a long time, the dean has no reason to suspect that a less altruistic motive subconsciously dictated his action. His relationship with Goody is an exemplary one between a medieval prelate and his humble parishioner. She is his "daughter in God,"[3] and when they chance to meet, she smiles shyly, "pausing to cross herself at his blessing." Then suddenly one day, when her red hair springs "so unexpectedly from the decent covering of the wimple," all that innocent time before is "wounded." The wound never heals properly: "the secure time"[4] is not restored; Jocelin becomes obsessed with "her hidden red hair."[5] He feels "the prurience in him like a leprosy."[6] Even prayer is to no avail. For "when he glanced up to where help had been, a fall of red, knotted hair blazed there."[7] Nonetheless, his self-control does not waver, and he keeps up appearances in his meetings with her until he tries to console her upon the death of Pangall, a death he has unwittingly caused. She shrinks from the proferred consolation, perhaps because she has begun to suspect, but he forces it upon her with this postscript: "And meanwhile—all these years—My child, you are very dear to me." Shocked, she retorts, "Not you *too!*" and flees, "gasping and sobbing."

Some people have experiences but miss meanings; others have meanings but miss experiences; a chosen few have both. Goody's arranged marriage to an impotent man covers the second. Jocelin's progress from ignorance to enlightenment about the sexual significance of the spire blankets the other two. Throughout most of the novel he epitomizes the first kind of person so that he reacts to Goody's recognition of his concealed lust, which he still refuses to comprehend, with anger and confusion: "What's all this?"[8] But in a sudden flash of perception at the end, he sees the spire as a phallic club rising up toward "a tangle of hair, blazing among the stars." And so at last, becoming consciously aware of the erotic aspect of his vision, he murmurs to himself: "That's the explanation. . . ."[9] Only after Goody is dead and Jocelin himself is on his deathbed is he able to admit that his ambition to erect the spire was connected to his interest in her. The spire originally conceived as a glorifying adornment for a house of God is turned into the outlet for long-repressed sexual yearnings. The spire become phallus, this self-uplifting for self-gratification, has been a substitute satisfaction for a desire that this medieval man of God must deny. *The Spire* is basically the story of how an erotic fancy is inadequately sublimated into a work of religious art. A few minutes later, this phallus-spire is joined by a prayer-spire. His death-clouded eyes envision the spire as "rushing upward to some point at the sky's end, and with a silent cry. It was slim as a girl, translucent. It had grown from some seed of rose-coloured substance that glittered like a waterfall, an upward waterfall. The substance was one thing, which broke all the way to infinity in cascades of exultation that nothing could trammel."[10] Ultimately he recognizes the dual nature of the spire as of this world, the color of human flesh, at the same time that it is not of this world, the color of the mystic rose.

Jocelin's ascent to humility and self-knowledge, from pride and self-delusion, is characterized by pain and travail both for himself and for those involved with him. His own suffering is clinical and emotional—clinical in that he contracts tuberculosis of the spine. Added to this is the anguish caused by revelations of a dark past. Foremost among these was his supposedly fatherly feeling for Goody. After this is called into question, a whole slumbering host of doubts arise: doubts about his vocation, the holy relic from Rome that he enshrines in the tower, and the integrity of the original builders of the cathedral. The first two rude awakenings are the work of his aunt and patroness, the Lady Alison, of whom he disapproves. A mistress of the late king, she reveals to Jocelin that he owes his rapid advancement in the church, including his deanship, not to divine preferment and his own merits as he always supposed, but to her intercession. She and the previous king, in a digression from lovemaking, chose Jocelin on a whim, plucking him from a monastery where he was a novice and earmarking him for a quick rise. This erstwhile courtesan also disillusions him as to "the Nail," that he assumed to be a relic of the true cross. In rapid sequence, he learns that the stone columns of the cathedral on which his tower depends are rubble-filled and that is why they sing in agony under the growing weight. With this discovery, an architectural stigma is visited upon him: Jocelin becomes the spire. He is "struck . . . from arse to the head with a white-hot flail. It filled his spine with sick fire and he shrieked because he could not bear it yet knew he would have to."[11] At this point, the monomaniac and the object of his monomaniacal vision fuse: his spine becomes as maimed as the spire, which, owing to the corrupt columns, has slipped twenty-three inches out of true perpendicular.

His own suffering, grotesque as it is, is exceeded by the hardship this visionary teetering on the edge of madness inflicts upon others. In the burst of self-enlightenment that accompanies his last days upon earth, he regretfully admits that "I traded a stone hammer for four people."[12] He alludes to two couples: Pangall and Goody and Roger and Rachel Mason. Jocelin blackmails Roger Mason, his aptly named master builder, into completing the precarious work, long after they discover that the foundation is inadequate to support the crushing weight of the mounting tower. Dispirited and sodden with drink, Roger, who opposes each stage of the construction, reluctantly goes on with the work and drifts into a liaison, born of desperation, with Goody. He eventually attempts suicide in an outhouse, which fails only because, ironically, he miscalculates the "breaking strain"[13] on a rafter. Rachel, barren because of an unfortunate giggle that renders coital fulfillment impossible, is driven to Ophelia-like distraction, and Goody dies horribly in an agonizing childbirth. But the most horrifying fate is Pangall's. The construction workers, forced to go on with the work, panic, turn on Pangall with rage, mock his manhood, sadistically slay him, and hurl him into the foundations.

In earlier novels, Golding was obsessed with the myth of the Fall, and, while there are vestiges of it here, central emphasis is placed on the nature of faith. I said earlier that the development of *The Spire* can be traced through Jocelin's growing awareness of the sexual significance of the spire. In a larger context, the development of the novel has to be traced through Jocelin's growing awareness of what it means to have faith. Faith and the human cost are the overarching theme. In the beginning, what Jocelin deems faith is merely the good face that he places upon his pride, stubbornness, and complacency. On the long-awaited day when the construction commences, he prays—if it can be called praying— "What can I do on this day of days, when at last they have to fashion *my* [italics added] vision in stone, but give thanks?" And he commissions a sculptor to carve four flattering likenesses of his head in stone for mounting on the completed tower. As he sits for the sculptor and listens to him tapping away, the dean exults, "Thou dost glorify the lives of Thy chosen ones, like the sun in a window." The reference to the sun and the stained-glass window sets the tone of the opening chapters. Sunlight and stained-glass windows, frequently alluded to in the first chapter, are the deceiving outward appearance of what he calls "my vision,"[14] sunny and rainbow-hued. But these initial allusions are not without a hint of the anguish and torment to come. The sunlight in the nave is trapped in choking dust stirred up by the workmen. And the stained-glass window of the opening paragraph depicts Abraham's readiness, at God's command, to offer Isaac, his only son, in sacrifice. Thus if Jocelin is blissfully unaware of the cost of faith at this point, the reader is not.

The self-exaltation phase is gradually replaced by one of doubt, the emerging realization that faith has been known to exact a toll. After repeated fallings out with his clerical colleagues—all of whom oppose him—over the construction of the tower which comes to be known derisively as "Jocelin's Folly," the dean muses: "I didn't know how much you would cost up there, the four hundred feet of you. I thought you would cost no more than money. But still, cost what you like."[15] When the cost first occurs to him, it does not seem prohibitive, but even when it does, it does not deter him in the least. He tells Roger: "I see now it'll destroy us of course. What are we, after all? Only I tell you this, Roger, with the whole strength of my soul. The thing can be built and will be built, in the very teeth of Satan."[16] Roger's every effort to dissuade him is in vain. Jocelin persists in what he knows to be his folly and makes light of the sacrifice: "I thought it would be simple. I thought the spire would complete a stone bible, be the apocalypse in stone. I never guessed in my folly that there would be a new lesson at every level, and a new power. Nor could I have been told. I had to build in faith, against advice. That's the only way. But when you build like this, men blunt like a poor chisel or fly off like the head of an axe. I was too taken up with my vision to consider this; and the vision was enough."[17] The vision was enough to make the "building of the spire an overriding necessity."[18]

Doubt and disillusionment, a long phase, are succeeded by the realization that deranged perseverance is not faith. Jocelin comes to perceive a pattern amidst the confusion: he sees his so-called vision has been "blasphemy." The glorification of God, he learns, has another less appealing name—self-aggrandizement. The gap between vision and reality is to blame. He explains this to Father Adam: The spire's "an ungainly, crumbling thing. Nothing like. Nothing at all."[19] In this sense, *The Spire* is a novel about the abyss between the anticipation and the fulfillment of an ideal. Jocelin's ordeal is not in vain, however. The trial by fire crumbles his pride; on his deathbed he has a true vision: only hell awaits pride. *"There is no innocent work. God knows where God may be,"*[20] Jocelin gasps in his newly found and hard-won humility. He arrives at the understanding that the spire is built on blood and sin, precisely because it is the work of man. Perhaps there is an implicit moral here: Golding may be reminding us that all men are sinners and that the good and the beautiful are necessarily created by sinners.

With scant hours to live, Jocelin makes the painful discovery that all along his fanatical pride has masqueraded as faith. Undaunted, despite almost unbearable physical suffering, he seeks to find in the hour of death what has eluded him down all the years, and suddenly—but not miraculously—he finds it. I say not miraculously, because the faith that he embraces is probably more secular than religious. Ironically, it is while he is being coaxed into a conventional gesture of assent by Father Adam, a priest about to confer the last rites, that he makes his own unconventional statement of faith. Instead of *"God! God! God!"* Jocelin's last cry is *"It's like the apple tree!"*[21] The apple tree, although it makes a belated and brief appearance in the novel, like the spire, is deep with levels of meaning, richly textured with ambiguities, and resonant with symbolic imagery. On one level, "it" refers to the spire: the spire is like the apple tree. Both are mixed gestures of assent, touching men and angels, earth and air, corruption and faith. On another level, life is the antecedent of "it": life is like the apple tree of man's knowledge and "free fall." A lengthy citation is necessary at this point in order to delve into the manifold implications of this very involved analogy.

En route to a hoped-for but not-to-be reconciliation with Roger Mason, Jocelin, walking only with the utmost effort, observes an apple tree replete with a vision of angels:

> There was a cloud of angels flashing in the sunlight, they were pink and gold and white; and they were uttering this sweet scent for joy of the light and the air. They brought with them a scatter of clear leaves, and among

the leaves a long, black springing thing. His head swam
with the angels, and suddenly he understood there was
more to the apple tree than one branch. It was there
beyond the wall, bursting up with cloud and scatter,
laying hold of the earth and the air, a fountain, a marvel,
an apple tree; and this made him weep in a childish way
so that he could not tell whether he was glad or sorry.
Then, where the yard of the deanery came to the river
and trees lay over the sliding water, he saw all the blue
of the sky condensed to a winged sapphire, that flashed
once.
     He cried out.
     "Come back!"
     But the bird was gone, an arrow shot once. It will
never come back, he thought, not if I sat here all day. He
began to play with the thought that the bird might return, to sit on a post only a few yards away in all its
splendour, but his heart knew better.
     "No kingfisher will return for me."[22]

This Garden of Eden perception of beauty defies a definitive
gloss. But if the evocations do not work on a discursive level,
they do on an experiential one where angels, "pink and gold
and white," are forced to consort "among the leaves" with a
snake, "a long, black springing thing."
     The kingfisher is counterpointed with a bluebird that Joce-
lin invokes in the course of his final testament.

What is terror and joy, how should they be mixed, why
are they the same, the flashing, the flying through the
panic-shot darkness like a bluebird over water? . . . In the
tide, flying like a bluebird, struggling, shouting, scream-
ing to leave behind the words of magic and incomprehension—
It's like the apple tree![23]

Both birds make an ephemeral flight over water which they
struggle to prolong. But the differences are more important.
The one flashes through a blue sky (hope is still uppermost);
the other wings "through the panic-shot darkness" (Jocelin's
death is imminent). The kingfisher leaves no legacy; the blue-

bird whirls out a mystery, a dark revelation full "of magic and incomprehension." The kingfisher resembles Hopkins' goldfinch—combining angelic gold with reptilic black—to a point: they attest to pied beauty, dappled faith, and the transience of any life-span. But unlike the goldfinch who helps Hopkins look homeward to heaven, the kingfisher performs no manifestly similar function for Jocelin, who complements his first choice with a bluebird.

The bluebird resembles Keats's nightingale: both birds provide fleeting night glimpses into an immortal truth about mortality. The poet and the dean, brooding over the difference between life as they know it and life as the birds know it, receive an unexpected revelation. Following Keats, Golding exploits the method of paradox. The linking of opposites is necessitated by the novelist's conception of beauty, beauty that makes demands on the entire emotional makeup and that allows sensitive minds to see joy and terror, life and death, faith and unfaith, as parts of an integral whole. The difference is in the reaction: the poet doubts the value of the "vision"; the dean considers it far more than only "a waking dream." The one, concluding that the realm of the nightingale is an illusion, slips back, exhausted and disappointed, into the world of pain and sorrow. Whereas the other, concluding that the excitement and insight that he has acquired in the realm of the bluebird is a perfectly valid transcendent experience, returns to the world of reality content to die with dignity and courage.

The implication is that Jocelin, in experiencing the bluebird's flight, has been in contact with some higher revelation about life and death. I have so far resisted the temptation to translate this imaginative analogy into conceptual terms, but perhaps a suggestion, as distinct from a full-dress explanation, is in order. The phrase "through the panic-shot darkness" surely connotes something concerning Jocelin's state of mind with death immediately imminent but less surely something concerning his destination. Life is a flash over water with panic at the end, "a whirl of terror and astonishment"[24] at the approach of the unknown, and perhaps a hint of light to come. This latter conjecture is consistent with Golding's Keatsian affirmation of joy in the midst of terror and with the allusion to the apple tree—the angelic blossoms exuding a "sweet scent for joy of the light." Add to this all the blue of the sky concentrated in the one-way flight of the splendidly plumaged kingfisher and the picture is one of the moment of transition from life to death as Jocelin comes to feel it.

This is no Apostles' Creed, and for a medieval priest Jocelin's semiagnostic credo is an anachronism, of course. But I suspect that it is Golding's own "I believe . . ." At the approach of death, Jocelin fervently expresses his creator's humanistic faith; even though for most of his life he has mouthed the traditional form of assent in the Middle Ages, theocentric faith. Roger Mason, the aspect of unfaith, constitutes the third angle in this triangular statement of faith. Humanistic faith having been explored, there is a need to examine briefly the remaining two.

Theocentric faith manifests itself throughout *The Spire* in terms of Biblical allusions. The novel opens with references to Abraham and Isaac as well as to Abel. The stained-glass window of Abraham and Isaac functions in a way similar to the pillar of Abel. The window looks beautiful and the pillar looks straight, but they tell a story of woe and crookedness. In a desecrating parallel, the murder of Pangall grimly parodies the Abraham and Isaac story. The pagan workmen defile the cathedral by offering a human sacrifice to the devil. After torturing Pangall obscenely, they ritually murder him and bury him in the pit beneath the crossways where, crossed with the Druidic devil-worshiping sign of mistletoe, he crouches in a perpetual vigil—an inverted mirror image of the sacrament of Baptism. The torment that Jocelin himself suffers after being forcibly ejected from Roger's room, his ears ringing with curses, reenacts not only Pangall's death but also Christ's rejection. As he crawls in the gutter, the mob —never identified but all the more sinister for that, recruited perhaps from irate parishioners and the irascible army of workmen—hound him with "imprecation and hate," pelt him with fists and feet and strip the clothing from his back. In imitation of the archetypal scapegoat, his only response is to cry out: "My children! My children!"[25] After a lifetime of preaching theocentric faith, he defers his practice of it until now, for the essence of this kind of faith is courage, willingness to trust, and, above all, willingness to be a fool for God. As Jocelin explains to Roger: "Even in the old days He never asked men to do what was reasonable. Men can do that for themselves. They can buy and sell, heal and govern. But then out of some deep place comes the command to do what makes no sense at all—to build a ship on dry land; to sit among the dunghills; to marry a whore; to set their son on the altar of sacrifice. Then, if men have faith, a new thing comes."[26]

Referring to the building of the tower, Jocelin would always say: "I am about my Father's business." He liked to think of himself as God's instrument for joining "earth to heaven," for making "geometric lines . . . leap into a picture of infinity."[27] Roger Mason, the master builder and his skeptical adversary, wary of miracles and short on divine trust, counters this upward vision by emphasizing the physical reality of the spire. As they stand on the parapet, he tells the dean: "Let your eye crawl down like an insect, foot by foot. You think these walls are strong because they're stone; but I know better. We've nothing but a skin of glass and stone stretched between four stone rods, one at each corner. D'you understand that? The stone is no stronger than the glass between the verticals because every inch of the way I have to save weight, bartering strength for weight or weight for strength, guessing how much, how far, how little, how near, until my very heart stops when I think of it. Look down, Father. Don't look at me—look down!"[28] He knows what he knows: the church rests on rubble and mud; the pillars are bent, groaning under the weight of the swaying spire which, having impacted itself crookedly in the parapet, gives every indication of tearing and splitting with the next windstorm. But the voice of reason is so terrified by the voice of "faith" —an idealist-villain progenitor of obsessive uncompromising earnestness, with an unconquerable will, who spares no one and nothing in his demonic zeal to erect the tower—as to be overwhelmed by it. Impotent to act, Roger despises Jocelin, the so-called man of faith who causes more intense suffering by his "faith" than the most talented doubting Thomas could with twice his opportunities.

Jocelin is not dead in life: he retains the potential for change and redemption. He replaces lip-service theocentric faith with a felt humanistic equivalent. His God-oriented "faith," sustained by lofty rhetoric but wanting in charity—with one obvious exception: his too brief turn-the-other-cheek display when visited with mob violence—was a charade; his man-oriented faith, characterized by self-panic, shame, and deeds of atonement, is his salvation. He has his special vision of love only when his hypocritical trust in God wanes and his sincere trust in man waxes—the mob violence scene is the cross-bearing climax of this internal upheaval. The hypocrisy in the God-centered stage of Jocelin's "faith" shows that Golding was not trying to be ironical when he wrote *The Spire*. Given this theme, the striving for irony would have been an irresistible temptation for Shaw, for example, but not for Golding: he is not putting down divine love and elevating human love as the route to salvation. He is demonstrating an irrefutable fact: bogus love of God is no match for authentic love of man. And remember that the mob violence scene with its implication of genuine love for God is the bridge between the two. The incoherent tremor of Jocelin's lips—*"It's like the apple tree!"*—which Father Adam misconstrues as *"God! God! God!"* is not such a mistaken interpretation after all. It is in accord with Jocelin's hard-earned realization that the supernatural must be approached by way of the natural, that God manifests himself solely through sensory-perceived creation. Hopkins' well-known sentiment, "The world is charged with the grandeur of God," is relevant here, except that Golding renders it less exultantly, more prosaically. For he has Jocelin reflect: "And what is heaven to me unless I go holding him by one hand and her by the other?" On the same occasion, "a grey, successive day for dying on,"[29] there is an even more pertinent reflection: "If I could go back, I would take God as lying between people and to be found there."[30] And so the theoretical distinction between theocentric faith and humanistic faith becomes at last almost a semantic one in this novel.

2

The Spire, with stress on the cost of faith, recalls Ibsen's play *The Master Builder* (1892), which stresses the cost of success. A middle-aged man's introspection about the nature of success in terms of other people's suffering is transformed into another middle-aged man's introspection about the nature of faith on the same terms. Both works are marinated with images and observations dealing with death and vanity. *The Master Builder,* rich, complex, and nearly inexhaustible, is Golding's great example. Jocelin's resemblance to Halvard Solness, the Master Builder, a specialist in erecting churches, is considerable. These demon-driven, self-deceived spire builders are sinners with a saintliness latent in their eleventh-hour thrust for martyrdom. To attain their ends, they manipulate people ruthlessly, and so they are freighted down with uneasy consciences. Both experience guilt which culminates in self-flagellating mortification; both are paranoidal and Promethean; both are destroyed by young women with irresistible sexual charm; and both undergo ambiguous deaths.

Jocelin shares a tyrannical nature with Solness. They treat other people as dehumanized objects, existing exclusively for their own use. Solness bullies his wife and keeps his employees down. A younger associate, a draftsman of considerable promise, for instance, is calculatingly discouraged and deliberately crushed. Solness clings to young people only to destroy them. Jocelin, as we have seen, bullies everyone who is even remotely connected with the construction of the spire, notably his architect (also referred to as the master builder, although Jocelin himself is the true master builder, for it is he who conceives the vision and drives the project on) whom he does not hesitate to blackmail when every other ploy designed to keep him on the job fails. Jocelin shares consciously idealistic aims with Solness, who began by building churches dedicated to the honor and glory of God. Both desire something intensely and are extremely rigid in the pursuit of that desire. Both are confused as to what they desire. They imagine their goal is to add to the extrinsic glory of God; in fact it is to aggrandize themselves boundlessly. They are thus more willful than truly idealistic.

In pursuing ideals to the point of destruction—in Shaw's words, Ibsen's major theme was "ideals . . . demand human sacrifices"[31]—these twin tower builders exhibit symptoms paranoidal and Promethean. Solness is neurotically fearful of the menace posed by the younger generation of architects and ridden with the anxiety that they are conspiring to oust him from his ascendant position. He is quite ecstatic when he is told he alone should be allowed to build, that all competition should be suppressed. The Master Builder's original intention was to construct churches and nothing else, but when God permitted his wife's home to be burnt and their children to be taken from them, all that changes. He pledges himself to divine defiance: never again to build a church; to concentrate on "homes for human beings"; in general to rival the "Mighty One . . . [as] a free builder."[32] The dean, too, likes to envision himself in conflict with a more than mortal foe. In the midst of all the difficulties, human and mechanical, attendant upon the erection of the spire, Jocelin vows that he shall prevail despite Satanic competition. "It's become a race between me and the devil. We're going faster, both of us, racing for the line. But I shall win."[33] And his implacable resolve to persevere in the work, against every man-made, natural, and demonic obstacle to the contrary, eventually shades into defiance of the Creator as implied by the last sentence of chapter eight: ". . . at the crossways, the replaced paving stones were hot to his [Jocelin's] feet with all the fires of hell."[34]

The play as well as the novel contains a protagonist who,

at one time, exchanges faith for disloyalty to God. In both instances, the irreverent lapse is attended by a young woman, whose very presence has a profoundly disturbing effect upon the hero, and a dollop of grievance. The Master Builder desires punishment to purge himself of the guilt he bears toward his long-suffering wife: a nagging sense of guilt born of the past personal tragedies he feels responsible for— the loss of their twin sons and their house in the fire. The opportunity for salutary self-torture presents itself in the form of youthful Hilda, a member of the generation he fears. Hilda reenters Solness' frustrated life after a long absence. Ten summers earlier, they had first met when he was building a tower on an old church in the mountain village where she lived. Despite the fact that she was only twelve or thirteen at the time, he apparently tried to seduce her, and he promised to return for her in a decade. When he fails to show, she, suitably dressed as a mountaineer, comes down for him. Her expressed motive is to be of use to him. This ethereal-appearing creature explains that she has selected him for a higher purpose. She had remembered him as a superior person, a kind of throwback to the noble Viking of old, but one who had not quite achieved his full potential. She seeks the Master Builder out to goad him into attempting "the impossible." But her repressed motive is revenge, as the bird of prey metaphors, so frequently associated with her, suggest. In other words, her unconscious attitude toward Solness is at variance with her conscious attitude, and this situation is reflected in Jocelin's ambivalence toward Goody —although the attitudes he is torn between are not an other-directed death wish and hero worship but rape and goodwill. In both pairings, the altruistic impulse conceals a hostile one, with the difference, of course, that Hilda is the victimizer while Goody—a far more passive creature, in keeping with what medieval custom decreed proper for a woman—is the victim. The sequence of deed and guilt is another difference. Solness is guilt-ridden before Hilda's unexpected reappearance and is unconsciously awaiting his own destruction. Jocelin's guilt load descends after the fact of the arranged mar-

riage between Pangall and Goody. It coincides with the
dean's belated discovery that his interest in the girl was carnal to begin with.

Hilda's unexpected visit and her whimsical-appearing but
actually baleful insistence that Solness keep his "promise"
and present her with "a castle in the air"[35] precipitates the
Master Builder's death. She is disappointed when she learns
that he no longer builds churches and church towers. But she
recovers her gaiety when she is told he has just completed a
new house with a tower for himself. At the dedication ceremony, she prevails upon him personally to climb with a
wreath to the top of the tower, even though she is aware of
his morbid fear of heights and susceptibility to vertigo—
symptoms shared by Jocelin and Roger, incidentally. After
hanging the wreath around the weather vane and waving to
the throng below, he loses his footing and is dashed to the
ground to the consternation of all the onlookers except Hilda,
who, greedily content with her triumph, is euphoric. His
spire-topping, spire-toppling death is the condition for her
fulfillment. This sexually fearful man who habitually used
other people to achieve his arrogant purposes is now used by
a sexually arrested girl to achieve orgasm. The circle is
closed. Solness' unalterable will to reach the top, literally and
figuratively, destroys him. To the extent that he remains
pathologically ambitious to the end, his death is negative: the
events leading to his disaster do not change him; it is even
doubtful that he learns anything about himself from them.
Jocelin's willingness to pay any price to attain his goal also
destroys him. But his death, owing to his change of heart
before "life's fitful fever is over," is more affirmative. In the
Oedipal tradition, Jocelin acquires insight and strength
through suffering; in the Medean tradition, Solness suffers in
vain.

As formidable as the human protagonists in these two
works are the tower and the spire. They signify physical
death in the mad pursuit of ideals and gigantic wish-fulfillment phalli; they also symbolize their creators' neurotic need
to isolate themselves from others in order to rise above

humankind and, where God is concerned, polarized postures of worship and defiance. The traditional references of the tower and the spire to ideals, sex, religion, solitude, and pride encourage these dazzling ambiguous ramifications. These brilliant conical images exact a cost, however: the characters remain convincing but scarcely realistic. Hilda and Goody appear partly to be projections of the egos of Solness and Jocelin, their ambitions and anxieties. The women plus the tower and the spire represent not simply the exhibitionistic tendencies of these men but the creative urge and the guilt these men have in common with other modern heroes—despite the medieval *mise-en-scène,* the character of Jocelin is modern in conception and execution. The dizziness Solness and Jocelin experience in ascent is that of achievement and conscience. To become "free builders," to reach the summit of success and faith, they must pay the price in sacrifice, offering up themselves, family, friends, and coworkers. But in their microcosmic reflection of the universal dilemma the artist confronts today, there is this difference: ultimately, Solness has to renounce the higher reaches of his art for the sake of popularity whereas Jocelin never falters, never compromises. The exiled, guilty, and all but frustrated artist in our time and the nature of his art have seldom been more impressively devised in character and image than in Golding's *The Spire.*

The Spire mediates most impressively between the temporal and the spiritual. So too does much of the fiction of John Updike. It is fitting that he should be our next stop.

3

John Updike

BETWEEN HEAVEN AND EARTH

1

In the course of an interview a few years ago, John Updike twice linked *The Poorhouse Fair,* his first novel, with *Couples,* his fifth. Both pose the same question. "As in *The Poorhouse Fair,* in this novel [Couples] I was asking the question, After Christianity, what?" Both contain echoes from the Bible. *Couples* "has the same ghostly relation to the Biblical story of Sodom and Gomorrah as *The Poorhouse Fair* did to the stoning of St. Stephen."[1]

It is curious that to date, at least to my knowledge, no critic has studied these two novels in the light of the author's response. I propose to do that on the assumption that it will illuminate them in a way that they have heretofore resisted.

First, with respect to *The Poorhouse Fair,* what does Updike envision as the successor to Christianity? Also, with respect to his first novel, what specific indebtedness is there to the New Testament account of the martyrdom of Stephen?

The Poorhouse Fair covers the events of a single August day, in the near future (ca. 1980), as they relate to the occupants of a rural poorhouse in New Jersey. It is no ordinary day but the day when the indigent aged hold their annual fair for celebration and profit at which they sell their handicraft and commodities—buns, cakes, candies, quilts, and small baskets filed from peach stones—to the townspeople, while a band on the porch plays Sousa's marches.

For a lean novel, the forefront characters are numerous. Conner, the youthful utopian-visioned superintendent—or, as he is called here, the prefect—who is regarded as a despot by the old folks, and Buddy Lee, his young assistant and lone friend, who is serving him as a kind of clerk-acolyte, represent the administration. The inmates are represented by their spokesman, John Hook, a keen-minded nonagenarian and longtime resident; William Gregg, a bilious personality and the fomenter of violence against Conner; George Lucas, a man with a chronic earache and a sick wife, Martha; Elizabeth Heinemann, a blind woman who spoke in "vowels . . . of different distinct colors, the consonants like leading in a window of stained glass"[2]; Amelia Mortis (significant name), a bald octogenarian with a goiter around her neck; and Tommy Franklin, who carves the world out of a peach stone. The novel, presenting as it does a violent, complex little world, a microcosm that mirrors the issues and tensions of a larger world outside, finds its embodiment in this old man. He is the parable made flesh.

The dramatic center of *The Poorhouse Fair* is a gripping confrontation between Conner and Hook. It is occasioned by a midday thunderstorm which, threatening to wash out the much anticipated fete, necessitates a council in the sitting room, a conclave that turns out to be both an exposure of and a judgment on the prefect. After a falling out over politics, they proceed to debate the existence of God and the problem of human suffering while the others form a neo-Greek chorus. Hook upholds the traditional Christian position; Conner the atheistic humanistic position. Conner argues that the creation of the world was an accident. "Imagine a blind giant tossing rocks through eternity. At some point he would build a cathedral."[3] Hook retorts: "It seems implausible. . . . I do not quite see how any amount of time can generate something from nothing."[4] Conner equates pain with evil and insists that it always interferes with individual fulfillment. Hook sees suffering as the opportunity for virtue and regards it as the indispensable condition for character growth. The debate crackles with genuine dialectics—reminiscent of a similar encounter between Settembrini and Naptha in *The Magic Mountain*—because Updike's sympathies are divided: his head rules in favor of Conner; his heart is for Hook. The truth is not in Hook nor in Conner but in the conflict between them.

The author does not view either of the antagonists as a mere convenience of argument, even if the old folks do. Initially, their sympathies are with Hook—he is one of them —and against Conner—he expects too much from them. As the argument heightens and Conner's manner becomes condescending, even cruel, their anger toward him mounts. Besides, an incident just prior to the clash has upset them profoundly. When Conner orders the destruction of a stray cat, old and disabled, they see him as a euthanasia threat—a threat not without foundation, since he had once wondered whether it was really callous or not to regard "mass murder as the ultimate kindness the enlightened could perform for the others [the aged and infirm]."[5] The poorhouse inmates plan to strike first. Implicitly they agree to gang up on him, and this introduces the climactic stoning of Conner, an incident only ostensibly the result of whiskey and boredom.

The relationship of this incident to the Biblical story of the stoning of Stephen, narrated in The Acts of the Apostles 7:54 to 8:1a, is puzzling at first glance, and one wonders why Updike insists upon it. The correspondence is far from exact: Conner is not stoned to death; he is barely bruised. More important: Why does the foe of Christianity, in this novel, suffer something like the fate of Christianity's protomartyr? But to look for an exact similarity is folly, since Updike merely says that the one bears a "ghostly relation" to the other—meaning that *The Poorhouse Fair* bears only a faint, shadowy semblance to the Biblical original.

Perhaps we should proceed by ticking off the resemblances. The sole knowledge we have of Stephen's life and death is recorded in The Acts of the Apostles, chs. 6 to 8, where we learn that this man, "full of faith and of the Holy

Spirit" (ch. 6:5), likely a Jewish convert to Christianity, and six others were ordained by the apostles as the first deacons of the church in Jerusalem. Their chief function was to provide for Christian widows in need. Conner's vocation, to support the poor, is a borrowing. The Acts, however, tell us nothing of Stephen's work as a member of the committee on social welfare but rather how he devoted his time to preaching and converting. Here is a second resemblance: we learn much about Conner's "missionary" activity among the poor inmates but next to nothing about his social service. When Stephen is brought to trial for alleged blasphemy by the elders of certain synagogues in Jerusalem, he speaks at length about the history of Judaism, stressing the roles of Abraham, Joseph, and Moses. He follows this up by saying that the Temple and the Mosaic law were temporary and were to give place when God introduced the Messiah. And he ends with a harsh rebuke to his judges. Note the surprising absence of self-apologia. One commentator explains that "in apostolic times the speech of the accused on trial did not defend himself so much as the cause that he supported and represented."[6] So with Conner: when on "trial" in the sitting room, he cites his vision of a clean ample future free of gods and pain.

A tally of what Updike has borrowed from Stephen and what he has rejected in fashioning Conner shows that his portrait is that of a Stephen concerned with the here and now, rather than the hereafter. Conner, following Stephen, is protesting an established order and carrying a new gospel for which he is prepared to lay down his life. He "yearned for some chance to be proven; he envied the first rationalists their martyrdoms and the first reformers their dragons of reaction and selfishness."[7] That Stephen and Conner are opposed ideologists is not important to Updike; their common life-style is. He subtly reinforces the point by the choice of a motto: "If they do this when the wood is green, what will happen when the wood is dry?"—words uttered by Christ during the procession to Calvary (Luke 23:31).

This enigmatic reflection was addressed to certain women

of Jerusalem who were weeping in compassion for Jesus. Regarding them as the mothers of a sinful people, he advises them: "Weep not for me, but weep for yourselves and for your children" (Luke 23:28). And then he adds the aforementioned adage, for which there is this convincing exegesis. "In the Scriptures, the just man is compared to the fruitful, green tree (cf. Ps. i). If we make 'they' personal, the meaning is: If the Romans thus treat one whom they consider innocent, what shall they do to those whom they consider guilty? Since the expression is proverbial, it seems more probable that 'they' should be taken impersonally. Then the meaning is: If I who am innocent suffer thus because of sin, what shall be the punishment of those who are guilty of sin?"[8] First Conner bears a "ghostly" resemblance to Stephen and now by implication to Jesus.

Again the analogy is loose; the old people consider Conner guilty, guilty because geriatrics is a penance for him. They view him as a self-punishing do-gooder who feeds them the cold tin plates of social progress when they hunger for the bread of understanding—a sort of Grand Inquisitor figure. Remember the inference that Hook draws: he displays not goodness but busyness. But there is no doubt that Conner views himself—and to a degree Updike shares the view—not only as innocent but as Christlike. In the wake of the stoning, he commands: "Forgive them."[9]

Earlier Conner recalls his impression at having seen his predecessor Mendelssohn in his coffin. From the look of the deceased, he concludes that "Mendelssohn had . . . thought of himself as God." He resents the former prefect for this and for the fact that the old people held him in awe. "Conner thought of no one as God"[10]—although Buddy treats him as such—except, on occasion, himself. He is convinced "that he was the hope of the world,"[11] and he is disappointed when the blind woman reminds him: "You can't take the world on your shoulders."[12] Conner likes to dwell on "the importance of his position"[13]; his vow "to bring order and beauty out of human substance"[14]; the location of his office—so little accessible that the aged residents accuse him of being in hiding—

high in the cupola of the mansion turned poorhouse; the magnificent view from the light-flooded cupola where he "worked unseen"[15]; his unflagging devotion "in the service of humanity." And even what few little regrets he has—his "agony,"[16] his ability to help others immeasurably without at the same time being able to please them, and the mockeries and betrayals he is subjected to—are not incompatible with, say, God the Son's mission on earth.

Updike then intends Conner to be explicitly a Stephen figure and implicitly a Christ figure. But, of course, he does not treat the archetype in the same respectful and reverential way that many an earlier novelist did—the Russian Orthodox Dostoevsky for one. Alyosha and Father Zossima, for example, are traditional Christ figures symbolizing resistance to the scientific rejection of religion. Updike, on the other hand, responding to the impact of the intervening psychological and sociological naturalism, vacillates between nostalgia for lost religious values and mockery of them through a perversion of Christian martyr imagery. Specifically, he vacillates between the deadly serious violent rejection of a hallowed Stephen and the sham tongue-in-cheek rejection of a secular Stephen. He creates a materialistic Christ and a materialistic Stephen, shorn of transcendent overtones, as social scapegoats concerned more with the here than the hereafter. After the fashion of Camus and the later Hemingway, Updike approaches the plight of man, at least in this novel, from the apparently antipodal poles of secular existentialism and traditional faith.

Before we proceed to an interpretation of *Couples* and its Biblical model, a lingering glance at a relevant passage in The Acts of the Apostles will clarify an otherwise inexplicable habit of one of the characters in *The Poorhouse Fair*. George Lucas is portrayed as "forever digging in his ear with a wooden match to keep an earache alive."[17] Why this particular foible, rather than another, the novel itself never explains. There is, however, a clue in the castigation that Stephen administers to his persecutors. "You stiff-necked people, uncircumcised in heart and ears, you always resist the Holy

Spirit. As your fathers did, so do you. Which of the prophets did not your fathers persecute? And they killed those who announced beforehand the coming of the Righteous One, whom you have now betrayed and murdered, you who received the law as delivered by angels and did not keep it." (Acts 7:51–53.) Stephen approved of circumcision so that the opening metaphor is derogatory: a false ear is like an uncircumcised penis. The likelihood that Updike had something like this particular conceit in mind—despite the fact that ears would be more suitable female images—is strong, considering how sexual or religious imagery is always obtrusive whenever Lucas is "deep in his ear."[18] With Freudian sophistication, Updike alters the image from "uncircumcised" ears to that of a man poking a matchstick in an itching ear. This, of course, modifies the contextual metaphor: the implicit term is now sexual intercourse. Actually the conceit is hermaphroditic.

At the insistence of Conner, godlike in his own eyes, Lucas reluctantly agrees to go to the infirmary for treatment. At this point, the microcosmic sexual intercourse image becomes laden with religious overtones. Dr. Angelo is the resident physician. (Recall that those with "uncircumcised" ears "received the law as delivered by angels.") He has a nurse, Grace. He is said to be "like a joking priest," and his office resembles a confessional. In the course of Angelo's examination of Lucas' ear, there are three homosexual images and a masturbatory one. After Angelo inserts "the nozzle of a brass funnel painfully deep into" the patient's head, Lucas, certain that his ear is badly off, fearfully conjures up the notion that it "would have to be lanced."[19] He is terrified: "the prick pierced all the layers of numbness right through to the ultimate, blue-hot sheet of pain that set the limit to suffering."[20] By way of medication to ease the irritation, Angelo applies a little zinc at the end of "a small rod of cotton-tipped wood . . . inserting the warm gray unguent with a careful twirling motion that tickled intimate turnings dangerously near, Lucas felt, seats of pain." This psychosexual analysis of Lucas' deep-seated ambivalent attitude toward homosexuality—conveyed entirely by artistic indirection, by evocative twin-leveled allusions—culminates in a narcissistic image. To specify "the location of the worst redness" Angelo "made a circle with his thumb and forefinger and with a finger of the other hand rubbed the wrinkly part of the thumb skin."

The "uncircumcised" ear undoubtedly caught Updike's fancy to a greater degree than the "uncircumcised" heart, but he does not neglect the latter wholly. Scanning Lucas' medical chart, Angelo observes a notation: dead upper molar "liable to abscess." He advises Lucas to make an appointment with the dentist, for it could very well be "a submerged infection . . . inserting poison into the bloodstream until the host suffers a coronary."[21]

2

In *Couples,* the time span is much greater: the later novel, much bulkier, covers the events of a year and a half (April 1963 to September 1964) in the lives of ten couples in the fictitious town of Tarbox, twenty-seven miles to the south of Boston. The novel explores the impact of multiple adulteries and two divorces on the interrelated lives of these hedonistic couples.

The most prominent couples are the two who become divorced, Piet and Angela Hanema and Ken and Foxy Whitman. The divorces are mostly the result of Piet's numerous extramarital flings, particularly with Foxy. In this sense, the book is about sex. In the aforementioned interview, Updike contended that "sex, gossip and games are the ways in which the couples relate to each other." But the book is also about religion. In the same interview, where he affirmed the "ghostly relation" of *Couples* "to the Biblical story of Sodom and Gomorrah," he indicated that "God does withdraw through the book." God's withdrawal from the society of Tarbox as promiscuity proliferates suggests that the enfeeblement of Christianity provides the proper climate for the new humanism to thrive. Again, in the same interview, the novelist added, "Sex, in its many permutations, is surely the glue, ambience, and motive force of the new humanism."[22] Freddy Thorne is the dark prophet who brings, with his pornographic library, the new gospel to Tarbox.

Hook and Conner are sufficient to flesh out the clash between Christianity and contemporary humanism in a novel as short as *The Poorhouse Fair*. But for a novel like *Couples*, almost three times as long and far more complex, the same ideological combat requires a dual confrontation. On one level, the antagonists are Piet and Freddy. "Freddy's atheism, his evangelical humanism"[23] threaten Piet's stern Calvinistic heritage. On the domestic front, the tension between Piet and his wife points up the same conflict. Angela, whose religion is psychoanalysis, fights her husband's effort to claim their two children for Christendom and blames him for the four-year-old's belief in immortality. "Wouldn't it be healthier to tell them the truth," she scolds Piet, "we go into the ground and don't know anything and come back as grass." But if she loses with Nancy, she wins with Ruth, the eleven-year-old, who sneers: "God is retarded. . . . He lets little babies die and He makes cats eat birds and all that stuff. I don't want to sing in the choir next fall."[24]

Sporadically, some of the other characters take sides, too. Georgene, wife to Freddy who thinks that God is death ("Death is being screwed by God"[25]), keeps anthropomorphic faith with her husband by hawking the tidings, "Haven't you heard, God's a woman?"[26] Foxy, however, downgrades the Almighty with less severity but more conventionality by conceiving of him as a happy old man. But, on another occasion, when she opts for the Eucharist as the most wonderful thing in the world, she gives succor to Christianity.

As in *The Poorhouse Fair*, in this novel there is also Biblical indebtedness—this time to the Old Testament. Tarbox in particular and the United States in general, according to Updike—"the couples were in my mind a microcosmic middle-class America"[27]—are the western hemisphere's Sodom and Gomorrah. Genesis, ch. 19, is our only source of information on the destruction of these two cities, and Genesis says their destruction was divine punishment for their evil ways. In Gen., ch. 18, God promised Abraham that he would spare the two cities if he could find so few as ten just men there. But having found only one, Lot, God saved him together with his family before he "poured down on Sodom and Gomorrah sulphur and fire" (Gen. 19:24).

Couples borrows many details from Gen., chs. 18 and 19. Tarbox stands to the south of Boston just as Sodom and Gomorrah stood to the south of the Dead Sea in the time of Abraham. The Dead Sea, however, is less the Biblical Boston than the inspiration for a motif: the games the couples play in order to exempt their lives from the laws of living. (Could the ten adulterous couples be the reverse of the ten just men required to stay divine wrath?) After all, one Biblical scholar describes the Dead Sea as "a malignant smear of water" that "supports no life." And he adds: "The region is oppressive and unhealthy, though when the Israelites first espied it from the heights of the mountains of Moab to the east, the sea's deceptively blue surface shimmering in the sun must have impressed them as it so easily does the modern traveler."[28] Tarbox too is deceptive from a distance: when viewed from the cupola of the Congregational Church in the heart of town, it appears to be basking in the sun of God's blessing. And this superficial impression is strengthened by a casual stroll through the town, where three streets of the business district are named Hope, Charity, and Divinity. The only sign that all is not what it seems, that after all Tarbox is not a quiet lovely town, is the total lack of trees on Hope Street.

Although Piet, who is the most incorrigible philanderer in town, is not Lot, he resembles him in several ways. Both have two daughters, and both have wives who look back in the midst of holocaust for a sign from the heavens. Lot's wife, for defying the express injunction of an angel of the Lord, was turned into a pillar of salt. Angela, a spectator at the apocalyptic fire that consumes the Congregational Church, is observed by her husband—from whom she is now separated—in the act of walking away from the fiery scene, to "turn once, white, to look back, and walk on, leading their virgin girls."[29] Considering that neither girl has reached puberty, the epithet is redundant unless it is intended to recall the daughters of Lot, older, of whom their father says: they "have not known man" (Gen. 19:8).

Lot, having sought safety with his two daughters in a cave in the hills, subsequently has offspring by them, although he was not altogether culpable, by reason of having been their dupe. Incest, which was abominated by the Hebrews above every other sin, is as common a failing in the Tarbox Sodom as it was in the original. Playing with his daughters, Piet sometimes becomes tumescent. Once, coveting one of his lesser concubines, he is shocked to find that he is on the verge of transferring his passion for her to "his elder daughter [who] was, though not yet as tall as Bea, of a size that was comparable."[30] This is not an isolated example. At least one other time he unconsciously interchanges his elder daughter with his mistress. While Ruth is rendering an unkind evocation of Foxy, Piet, drunk, observes in silence how his daughter's figure is becoming so lithe and tall—striking qualities of Foxy's. A pun, "his tall cockpit,"[31] then crosses his mind. To be sure, it is consciously predicated of his mistress, not his daughter, but still there remains that hint of confusion in the mind of this father-lover. And crouching beside Ruth's bed of an evening, Piet holds her sleeping hand and muses: "I am your only lover. All who follow echo me."[32] Ruth, in turn, encourages him. Whenever Nancy and Angela disparage him, which is not often, she always takes his side: in "baby talk . . . her impulse of love sought disguise."[33]

In Tarbox, preoccupation with the incestuous impulse is not restricted to Piet and Ruth. At least two of the couples —the Applebys and the Smiths, contracted to "the Applesmiths" on account of their notorious spouse-swapping—find it fascinating. Janet Appleby recalls a near-incestuous encounter with her brother; her husband thinks that what is good for sibling cats must be good for human siblings. Marcia Smith rallies history to the defense of inbreeding: "Those pharaoh types married brothers and sisters right and left and there were no pinheads produced. So I think all this fear of inbreeding is Puritanism."[34] When he tires of playing it straight, Updike parodies the taboo in the person of Janet who is undergoing psychoanalysis. Having told her analyst of her mother's rejection of her and her father's pharmaceutical firm, she complains to the rest of the Applesmith ménage of his interpretation. "Every time I take a pill I'm having intercourse with my father, it's his seed." An analysand's dream, when confronted with such an analytical absurdity, is her retort. "What am I supposed to do when I get a headache and need two aspirin, dial a prayer?"[35]

That Updike intends a parallel between Sodom and Gomorrah and the United States is painfully clear when Piet moans: "God doesn't love us any more. He loves Russia. He loves Uganda. We're fat and full of pimples and always whining for more candy. We've fallen from grace."[36] At the height of the Cuban debacle, Piet anticipates God's fiery judgment momentarily in the form of Russian bombers. "Chicago and Detroit would go first. . . ."[37] The actual judgment comes near the end of the novel when the Congregational Church is burning and he thinks, "God's own lightning had struck it."[38] That Piet is a spokesman for the author, on these occasions, cannot be doubted in view of Updike's assurance that the conflagration symbolized "God having removed his blessing from America."[39] The church steeple is tipped with a five-foot colonial rooster. "Children in the town grew up with the sense that the bird was God. That is, if God were physically present in Tarbox, it was in the form of this unreachable weathercock visible from everywhere."[40] The weather vane turns out to be beyond the reach of the flames even: "the charred skeleton of the burnt church [is] topped by an untouched gold rooster."[41] To reinforce the parallel, the novelist makes one of the couples Jewish. Visiting the Saltzes, "Piet tried to tell them how he felt, especially in the society of Tarbox, as a sort of Jew at heart."[42] And, more explicitly, reflecting on Foxy's philo-Semitism, he thinks that she would have preferred "Abram [sic] over Lot."[43]

Foxy's mother finds Freddy "fascinating on modern psychology and myths."⁴⁴ Updike is also fascinating on these subjects. They form the major strands woven into the tapestry of *Couples*. If mythology, the "ghostly relation" of the novel to the Bible, is the warp; modern psychology, the proclivity of these highly introspective couples for analyzing one another, is the woof. To lace the insights of modern psychology into the contemporary novel is, of course, no innovation. The variation that Updike introduces successfully is not to insinuate them—the practice of most so-called psychological novelists—but to make the insights overt. In the interview, he explained that "the ménages in the book are meant to be seen within the large ménage, of people who know each other, who are asked to know each other *really*, to accept and forgive each other in an almost psychoanalytical way. Friendship edges into group therapy."⁴⁵ Many of the characters are psychoanalysts without portfolio who spend much of their time analyzing the motives that propel themselves and the remaining characters into the game of rotating beds. Employing psychological jargon and clinical labels can be potentially dangerous; it can clamp the novel in a case-history straitjacket. *Couples* escapes this unfortunate fate through Updike's skill. Three or four characters are in analysis so that it is natural for them to spout Freudian terminology. To a lesser degree so do the rest, but this can be justified by their generally high educational level; their intellectual pretensions, their cultural savvy, and their desperate need to understand their pitiable hedonism. In short, given the kind of characters the novelist chooses, their analytical orientation is not unseemly. Besides, he uses it for irony: at the beginning of the novel, Janet announces to the others, "I think we're the prettiest unselfconscious town in America."⁴⁶

Freddy Thorne, a dentist who wanted to be a psychiatrist but flunked medical school, is the local Freud. His is not a frontal attack, however: he ministers to a sick town by way of his role as games master. People laugh at him; he appears from one vantage point to be the recipient of a transplant from the village idiot. This clumsy, eloquent buffoon is like the clown whose lifelong ambition is to play Hamlet. He meditates on "the fate of them all, suspended in this one of those dark ages that visits mankind between millennia, between the death and rebirth of gods, when there is nothing to steer by but sex and stoicism and the stars."[47] He contends that the most wonderful thing in the world "is the human capacity for self-deception."[48]

He is headshrinker, sorcerer, philosopher, and priest to the couples. He fills them with "real gut talk" and plays "the great game of truth"[49] with them. At first he spreads encouragement: he counsels the couples to think of themselves as "a magic circle of heads to keep the night out," to make "a church of each other,"[50] to form "a conspiracy to protect each other from death,"[51] and to use what wisdom they have "to wave the smell [of death] away." He appears to be the Tarbox Dylan Thomas braying: "Do not go gentle into that good night." Unfortunately Freddy does not practice what he preaches. He does not "rage against the dying of the light." Far from affirming life while dying, he worships death. Later his preaching even changes and comes into line with his practice. Then he advises the couples to accept the fact that "you're born to get laid and die, and the sooner the better," and to recognize the truth that "to live is to lose."[52] The smell and hurt of love terrifies him. For all his frank talk with women and his countless invitations to seduction, he has "no serious physical intention: the verbal intimacy of gossip satisfied him."[53] His preference for coital conversation in lieu of coitus is explained by his description of Foxy's abortion, "pelvic orthodonture."[54] He lives in a fantasy world of terrifying women who when they do not have teeth in their vaginas have fire. "He [Freddy] had kept a half-measure of firmness, but the slick warmth of her [Angela's] vagina singed him like a finger too slowly passed through a candleflame."[55] No wonder he has a horror of castration, is psychologically impotent and settles for self-abuse. Freddy's sad lewdness has nothing to offer the couples. He is "a vortex sucking them all down with him."[56] Posing as a therapist, he lectures to them on mental health and the good life at a time when his own life and mind are being hopelessly shredded. They sit at his feet, listening to his initial advocacy of the good life devolve gradually into a dirge: Do not hope for anything at all from life.

The turnabout in Freddy's preaching—his acknowledgment of a subreligious gesture of surrender to death—occurs during his dry adultery with Angela, three quarters through the book, when he confesses: "Death excites me. Death is being screwed by God. It'll be delicious."[57] Here is the turnabout: a man who seems to want to make love reveals that he actually wants to be made love to. By equating God with death, he divulges his true intent: to make hate. Angela reacts by reflecting on the difference between her husband and this would-be lover: the one fights death; the other woos it. Freddy further embellishes the difference and by doing so becomes the first of three cuckolds to offer an explanation for Piet's prodigious mistress-mastery. Freddy alleges that of the men in their circle, Piet is the only real heterosexual. The other men, Freddy sees as either spoiled priests or homosexuals once removed who "screw each other's wives because they're too snobbish to screw each other." Himself he sees as the worst homosexual of all. "I want to be everybody's mother. I want to have breasts so everybody can have a suck. Why do you think I drink so much? To make milk."[58]

According to Ken Whitman, Piet the prime stud has a warped nature. "Behind all this playfulness you *like* to destroy. You love it. The Red-haired Avenger. You're enjoying this; you've *enjoyed* that girl's [Foxy's] pain."[59] The third cuckold to assess Piet's sexism pronounces a totally different verdict. Matt Gallagher, his business partner, tells him that his weakness is a tendency to let things happen, not to make decisions. Virile, sadistic, passive, are the three different ways that he appears to three different people. These glimpses, "as bizarre as the sight in a three-way clothing-store mirror of your own profile,"[60] reveal an admixture of fidelity and distortion. Freddy indulges in wish-fulfillment projection; Ken and Matt in displacement. Freddy would gladly barter his orphic preoccupations for Piet's skill in chas-

ing women into bed. Piet is Freddy's surrogate adulterer. He
represents the phallic fantasy of the man butting into middle
age: a lady on the hour, every hour. In the words of Freddy,
Ken is as "anal as hell"[61]: he has his own hang-up about
destroying people. He obstinately refused to impregnate
Foxy in the first few years of their marriage, despite her
desire for a baby. Matt transfers his uneasy feeling about
himself, that his wife is making decisions for him and he is not
calling the shots anymore, to Piet.

Their motives in reaching the conclusions they do about
Piet are one thing; the accuracy of their conclusions is another. The accolade that Freddy bestows upon Piet—the sole
heterosexual male among the couples—does not stand up
under scrutiny. Freddy's analysis of the males in the group
is exaggerated to begin with. There is no concrete evidence
of overt homosexuality among them and only flimsy evidence of a covert relationship between two of them. So it is
a question of relative potential; Piet's homosexual compo-
nent is as well developed as any. On at least two occasions,
he identifies himself explicitly with a woman. Describing his
showdown with the Whitmans to Freddy, "Piet felt fondness,
the fondness a woman might feel toward her priest or
gynecologist or lover—someone who has accepted her
worst."[62] (Incidentally, this sentence reads very like one of
Graham Greene vintage.) Trying to talk Angela out of a divorce action, "he fought against her as a raped woman might
struggle."[63] And it is questionable that he really likes women,
apart from their mother-surrogate function. When asked
why he never carries on with single girls, he replies: "I only
like married women. They remind me of my mother."[64] Said
in jest? Perhaps. Even so sometimes—Romeo to the contrary
notwithstanding—he jests at scars that has felt a wound.
When Piet has a nightmare, he wakes Angela up that she may
put her arms around him. She guesses the truth. She tells
him, "You sleep with women when you're really trying
to . . . bring her [his mother] back to life."[65] He needs mother-
ing. He tells Foxy, "I love you as a mother."[66] And he proves
it. Huddled in the bathroom with her during a party, Piet

begs Foxy, whose breasts are milk-laden after the birth of her baby: "Nurse me. . . . Nurse me."[67]

On the other hand, Piet Hanema does possess the knack of making a woman feel proud when he sleeps with her. Georgene testifies to this. "Only Piet had brought her word of a world where . . . every woman was some man's queen."[68] The truth about him is complex: Hanema is the coward and the embracer of life. (The Greek word means both.)

Ken's charge that Piet likes to inflict pain on others is reasonable on the surface. After all, he does have his bellicose moments in the midst of lovemaking: he slaps Bea Guerin and expectorates on her and punches his wife. But cruelty is not a customary accessory to his lovemaking, even though he discovers to his surprise that it is "a method to prolong the length of time . . . that he could inhabit a woman." Only when he is frightened does he bully women. More often he is gentle with them; usually he philanders as a convenience to inflict psychological torment upon himself. The desire for adultery is the mainspring for the feeling of guilt which has him wound up so tight. Foxy, who also plays the game of what makes Piet tick, sizes up his guilt complex thus: "You're very Puritan. You're quite hard on yourself. At first I thought you fell down stairs and did acrobatics to show off. But really you do it to hurt yourself. In the hope that you will."[69] Foxy is more perspicacious than her husband.

When having an affair, Piet is ambivalent: he wants to conceal it from his wife; yet he wants to confess his misery to her too. His secret turns into a rage to punish himself. He wants to hurt himself to atone for the complicity he experienced in the death of his parents. They were killed in an automobile accident on a night when he had been out tomcatting. He holds himself responsible, as though he were an accomplice to murder. Only rarely does he make his mistresses and his wife suffer because his parents were killed; mostly he makes himself suffer. His guilt is just excessive enough to make him want to lead a precarious life but not enormous enough to make him want to plunge to the bottom. "Piet yearned to peer into the chasm, to spy out the face of catastrophe."[70] But during the course of an affair, he once in a while loses his footing and descends into hell where his paramours are his demons. He is unable to have a woman without remorse. "His fornication [sic] with Foxy rose burning in his throat like the premonition of vomit."[71]

Piet's guilt feelings extend to Angela too. When Foxy is condescending toward her, he is displeased. "He did not like Angela to be dismissed. He felt his mistresses owed it to him to venerate her, since he had taken it upon himself to mock her through their bodies."[72] With so much guilt on so many different fronts, the punishment, soon or late, inevitably comes as a relief. He makes no effort to deny Ken's accusation. "It pleased Piet to be able to talk about it," and "he waited happily to be crushed, and dismissed."[73] Nature is merciful: she swiftly metes out the sought-after judgment. No sooner does he emerge from the confrontation house than "he stepped sideways into the pruned lilacs and was stabbed beneath an eye, and wondered if he were drunk, and thus so elated."[74]

Matt's theory as to what makes Piet run from bed to bed is not so accurate as Foxy's, but it comes closer to the mark than either Freddy's or Ken's. Piet is passive but in a more metaphysical sense than Matt allows. Piet is passive only in the sense that he has a death wish instead of a life wish. Sex is his sole and pitiable shield against the awareness of death. The motive that impels his chain wenching is an irrational desire to halt time in flight—more than that, to recapture the past—and so ostensibly to defer death, but actually this attitude merely postpones living. When he drives by old stately homes in town, he becomes "nostalgic for when he had never been."[75] He displays regressive fetal potential, whenever the world threatens to close in on him. When he first takes Foxy, she is four months pregnant with her husband's baby, and throughout the pregnancy their lovemaking is frenzied, but as soon as the baby is born, Piet's ardor cools. He tries to explain: "I was in you so deep, loved you so terribly, I'm scared of getting back in. I think we were given it once and to do it all over again would be tempting fate."[76] Is he talking about resuming a love affair or regressing to the maternal womb? Sometimes Piet indulges in part embryo-envy and part insect-wish projection as when he sees Bernadette Ong's "dying husband in her like a larva in a cocoon."[77] Wombs and tombs: like Dylan Thomas, Piet barely knows the difference. Whenever he copulates, it is always the same: "in a manner analogus to dying he had trespassed into a large darkness." Still, paradoxically, the pressure of libidinous desire also momentarily eases the pain of death.

Piet's adulterous adventures are least perilous with sterile Bea. "His semen could dive forever in that white chasm and never snag."[78] Inside her forever vacant premises, "death no longer seemed dreadful."[79] Where life is barred, death seems remote. His adulterous adventures are most perilous with fertile Foxy, who takes no contraceptive precautions. He impregnates her just weeks after she has borne her husband's child. In her "silken salty loins he [Piet] had planted seed that bore his face." And again the womb becomes the *mise en scène* of a tomb encounter and infantile regression-aggression. "Now he wished to be small and crawl through her slippery corridors and, a murderer, strike."[80] Piet regards his orgasm with Bea simply as a stay against death. Whereas with Foxy his orgasm sets far more complex events—events in which death predominates—in motion: the ejaculation is Elizabethanly a little death for him, a little life for her, and ultimately death by abortion for the fetus.

Of all Piet's self-appointed amateur analysts, Foxy is the best. She serves him in the dual capacity of headshrinker and sexpot—an unusual combination. In a love letter, she reminds him "that man is the sexiest of the animals and the only one that foresees death." She sufficiently shares his qualms about mortality to add a P.S.: "After weeks of chastity I remember lovemaking as an exploration of a sadness so deep people must go in pairs, one cannot go alone."[81] (Here is another Graham Greene-like sentence. The incidence of them is surprising considering the wide divergence in style between Greene and Updike generally.) She provides him with insight not only on the Eros-Thanatos hang-up, but she

alone perceives that his fear of death is related to his ambivalent attitude toward religion. In another philosophical love
letter, she spys out his weakness: "You despise the faith your
fear of death thrusts upon you."[82] In other words, he despises
what he nonetheless needs in order to keep hope alive—a
belief in immortality. As Updike pointed out, Foxy and Piet
"are the only orthodox Protestants in the book."[83] Perhaps it
takes one to understand one.

Sex and death, death and religion, religion and sex are the
interwoven themes in the novel. I began my treatment of
Couples with the final pair. I should like to revisit the subject
by way of valediction.

Freddy Thorne with his anxiety about his manliness and
his talent for profanation invariably links the two, however
unsuitable the occasion. Hosting a party the night of Presi-
dent Kennedy's assassination, he converts carving a ham into
a mock oblation. " 'Take, eat,' he intoned, laying each slice
on a fresh plate a woman held out to him. 'This is his body,
given for thee.' " The guests reproach him for being disgust-
ing and wonder if fasting would not be more appropriate. His
almost instinctive reply, "Fasting or fucking,"[84] is typical of
his inability to distinguish between self-denial and self-indul-
gence. Allusions to intercourse and liturgy: the blend is characteristic of his response to catastrophe. At an earlier party,
when the other guests are expressing shock at the *Thresher*
submarine disaster, he automatically applies his formula.
"What shocked you about it? . . . They enlisted. We've all
been through it. . . . We took our chances honeymooning with
Uncle, and so did they." When he proposes a toast—"For our
gallant boys in the *Thresher*"—and is rebuked for it, his
apology is *"Mea culpa, mea culpa."* Unable to resist the
formula, once started, he adds: "You wonder what they
think. . . . The goddam gauges start spinning, the fucking
pipes begin to break, and—what? Mother? The flag? Jesu
Cristo? The last piece of ass you had?"[85] The others drown
him in their contempt. He provides the rallying point the
couples need, someone to despise, and they in turn provide
an outlet for his need, punishment. Freddy is the modern

scapegoat whose blasphemy and pornography are Puritanism turned inside out.

Piet proves to be an apt pupil of Freddy's. In church on Palm Sunday studying the altar cross, he wonders "if Freddy Thorne were right in saying that Jesus was crucified on an X-shaped cross which the church had to falsify because of the immodesty of the position." And "prayer and masturbation had so long been mingled in Piet's habits that in hearing the benediction he pictured his mistress naked."[86] He prefers a guiltless woman, the better to supply him with absolution for his marathon adulteries which are clearly associated with his spiritual confusion. Against marriage as a sacrament, he sets his own view: adultery in the presence of a third party is a sacrament. "You know what would seem like a sacrament to me? Angela and another man screwing and me standing above them sprinkling rose petals on his back." This voyeuristic fantasy addressed to Matt Gallagher evokes a Freudian interpretation: "As you described that I pictured a child beside his parents' bed. He loves his mother but knows he can't handle her so he lets the old man do the banging while he does the blessing."[87] The fantasy and the explanation are informative and shed considerable light on Piet's urgent desire to connect sex and religion. He underwent a traumatic experience when as a child it is likely that he witnessed parental lovemaking, but the fantasy disguises this as complaisant cuckoldry. To assuage the double guilt, this crypto-Puritan unerringly gropes toward the respectability provided by religion. To Foxy's insight, "You despise the faith your fear of death thrusts upon you," we may add, You despise the faith your feeling of shame in the presence of the body thrusts upon you.

Freud said in effect that lovemaking is usually not restricted to the two participants—that the unconscious usually summons a parent, a child, or some other third party to the bedside. Piet's funny prickly fantasy lends credence to Freud's contention that lovemaking is also a spectator sport. Children sprinkle blessings on a hairy back so that, in a fashion undreamed of by Milton, "they also serve who only stand

and wait." But when Piet's remorse mounts to a certain point
and compels him to break off the affair, then the children—
active spectators no longer—are transmogrified into active
participants. Trying to disentangle himself from Foxy, he
conceives a strategic metaphor. "They had been let into
God's playroom, and been happy together on the floor all
afternoon, but the time had come to return the toys to their
boxes, and put the chairs back against the wall."[88] If adultery
is a game played by children, a game moreover pleasing in
the sight of God, then there is no mess; no one is hurt; no one
has regrets; no one is stultified by guilt, and parting is just
sweet, never sorrow or even sweet sorrow. That this metaphor has not quite the charm to soothe the savage breast,
however, may be seen in two particulars. The terminology is
telltale: "playroom" (bedroom), "floor" (bed), "toys" (phalli),
"boxes" (vaginas). The equivalencies are self-defeating: the
act of returning "the toys to their boxes" is more in keeping
with a desire to resume the affair.

Piet, however, persists in trying to find his salvation in
metaphors. Sometimes he goes beyond merely invoking
God's blessing on adultery as in the nursery analogy. For
instance, what theodicy could be more bizarre than his in-
struction to Foxy: "God is right there, between your legs."[89]
Piet stops short of composing a litany—Vagina of Foxy,
glorify me / And defend me from mine enemies, etc.—probably only because his imagination deserts him. In any case,
his intention is obvious: O divine adultery! And his accomplishment is a breakthrough; he clearly outdoes his literary
precedents. Dante, for all the ecstatic ardor induced in him
by Beatrice, would undoubtedly have had serious reserva-
tions about installing his Paradiso in such dark cramped quarters. And how timid was D. H. Lawrence in locating the soul
or a minor divinity in the female genitals. Oral encounters
between Piet and Foxy are especially bathed in reverence.
Using a floral analogy, with funereal overtones, he insists that
cunnilingus is the latest theological fad. "To eat another is
sacred. I love thee, Elizabeth [Foxy], thy petaled rankness,
thy priceless casket of nothing lined with slippery buds."[90]

It afforded Piet solace to have thought of his parents as having been illiterate about sex. "I didn't think they knew a thing about sex," he confides to his wife, "and was shocked once when my mother in passing complained about the spots on my sheets. She wasn't really scolding, it was almost kidding. That must have been what shocked me."[91] That his mother might have had a sense of humor about sex was what made it all so unbearable for the teen-age Piet, and he shunted from his mind the implication that this couple, his parents, enjoyed coupling. Even into manhood he tormented himself periodically, wondering whether he had ever seen his mother naked. From this vantage point, Piet's compulsive adulteries are Puritanism in reverse.

In *The Poorhouse Fair* and *Couples*, Updike depicts the post-Christian time in which his characters live. The Christian myth is dead or dying, and they are awaiting something new. The elderly inhabitants of the poorhouse cling to the lingering traces while Conner, the prefect—rejoicing over the dead gods and conspicuously leaving their graves untended—baits them with the assassin, humanism. The more youthful inhabitants of Tarbox kick over the traces gleefully, using sexual promiscuity and assorted hedonistic conduct to celebrate the finish of the old Christian morality and to prepare the way for the new psychedelic morality. The new myth does not appear in *The Poorhouse Fair*, but it makes a belated appearance in the last pages of *Couples* where it is recorded in the form of experiments with LSD by the couples' successor, a new wave of younger, drug-oriented hedonists. Actually, *Couples* is a kind of elegy for the Protestant upper middle classes.

The demise of religion causes Updike greater alarm in the latter novel. In *The Poorhouse Fair*, he wavers between bestowing a wreath and declaring good riddance. In *Couples*, where he implies that we have not the strength to do without God, he suggests the need mankind has for religion and miracles—assuming that the untouched weather vane riding high over the gutted house of God is intended as one—even though they disappoint us. His indictment of the present, the unmistakable implication that America is heading for catastrophe, contains a plea for the special virtues of the past. This change in attitude from indecision to regret over the failure of religion can be accounted for by a religious crisis that he passed through in 1960. He got through it only by turning his back on the notion advanced by Conner that the nonexistence of God is reasonable. Unlike Conner, and for that matter unlike his black humorist colleagues, Updike was free from that moment on to hope for both the reality of God and the sanity of society.

Speculations on the vigor of God and spiritual crises in the midst of frenzied and often joyless sexual strivings characterize these two novels of Updike. To an even greater degree, these same demons populate the plays of Tennessee Williams. A Williams' census follows.

4

Tennessee Williams

GOD, SEX, AND DEATH

In the plays of Tennessee Williams, the enfeeblement of sex is exceeded only by the enfeeblement of God. The most felicitous simulacrum of this occurs in his 1972 play, *Small Craft Warnings,* when a hooker who has just "jerked off" a client is said to have God in her hands. This is typical: Deity reductionism is rarely conducted independently of sex—except in the instance of a few minor characters. But to study the phenomenon better, I plan to isolate it at the outset.

Chicken, the protagonist in Williams' one-act play, *Kingdom of Earth,* cannot make up his mind about God. First, referring to the sound of the flooding river swelling "to a muted lionlike roar," he says, "If God had a voice that's the way it would sound." Then, referring to the rumor that a neighbor who lives above him is preparing to dynamite his south-bank levee to save his north-bank levee with the strong possibility that the action will deluge Chicken's homestead, he adds, "Mr. Sikes is like God, he's got more to think about than people below him."[1] Without being aware of it, Chicken is trembling between two delicate theological conditions: anthropomorphism and anthropocentrism.

"All poets look for God,"[2] declares Mrs. Venable, a character in *Suddenly Last Summer.* Perhaps, but few look as strenuously as Tennessee Williams, and, like most creative writers, he conducts his search through his characters. Beginning with Chicken, a recent quester, and going back to Alma Winemiller, his earliest God seeker, there is consensus, if little orthodoxy, among his characters on the subject. Alma, a minister's daughter in *Summer and Smoke*, confuses the Almighty with a box of morphine tablets. "The prescription number is 96814. I think of it as the telephone number of God."[3] In the whole Williams' canon, *Camino Real* best illustrates this general agreement of opinion—despite an occasional surface disparity—on the present state of God. For the Survivor, God is a moron. "When Peeto [a pony] was 1-year-old he was wiser than God."[4] The Gypsy thinks of him as an unfeeling superscientist. "We're all of us guinea pigs in the laboratory of God."[5] In Esmeralda's eyes, the world has administered a sedative to God. "There has been so much of the Mumbo Jumbo it's put Him to sleep."[6] In the view of Kilroy, the Divine Creator has become an object of compassion. "I pity the world and I pity the God who made it."[7]

In *Suddenly Last Summer*, God is put down even further. Sebastian, the sybaritic poet, evolves a terrible, cruel image of God. He finds him after a long search, for the first time, at the moment he observes, from the crow's nest of a schooner off the Galapagos Islands, the spectacle of thousands of carnivorous birds devouring thousands of just hatched sea turtles. When he comes back down the rigging, his mother, Mrs. Venable, reports that he said, " 'Well now I've seen Him!'—and he meant God."[8] His cousin, Catharine Holly, expresses her confusion about God by repeating E. A. Robinson's well-known metaphor. "We're all of us children in a vast kindergarten trying to spell God's name with the wrong alphabet blocks."[9] The simile employed by the author in describing an action of Mrs. Venable, exposing as it does her invincible complacency as well as her confused notion of transubstantiation, is less telltale about the contemporary human condition in relation to God. Reverently approaching a copy of her dead son's vanity-published poetry, "she lifts a thin gilt-edged volume from the patio table as if elevating the Host before the altar."[10]

Boss Finley, the loathsome Southern demagogue in *Sweet*

Bird of Youth, frequently has delusions about his own
divinity. Alluding to his having been hanged in effigy on
Good Friday, he boasts: "I saw that was Good Friday. Today
is Easter Sunday and I am in St. Cloud."[11] On other occasions,
when modesty is more profitable, he is content to proclaim
himself a prophet. "When I was 15, I came down barefooted
out of the red clay hills. . . . Why? Because the Voice of God
called to me to execute this mission."[12] The Heckler, his
prime antagonist, far from being on such intimate terms with
God, announces that God is incommunicado. "I believe that
the silence of God, the absolute speechlessness of Him is a
long, long and awful thing that the whole world is lost because of. I think it's yet to be broken to any man, living or
any yet lived on earth,—no exceptions, and least of all Boss
Finley."[13]

In *The Night of the Iguana,* the personal idea of God held
by the Rev. T. Lawrence Shannon, a minister locked out of
his church for heresy and fornication, is a kind of muddled
pantheism. "I want to go back to the Church and preach the
gospel of God as Lightning and Thunder . . . and also stray
dogs vivisected and . . . and . . ."[14] A very different idea of
God is subscribed to by his congregation. He shouts at them
from the pulpit: "All your Western theologies . . . are based
on the concept of God as a *senile delinquent* and, by God, I
will not and cannot continue to conduct services in praise
and worship of this."[15] Hannah Jelkes, his spinster companion, is unsure about God. He is vaguely associated with the
white light she finally perceives "at the end of a long black
tunnel"[16]—the image she uses to describe her agonizing
journey through life.

The Milk Train Doesn't Stop Here Anymore is intended to
be an allegory on man's need for someone or something to
mean God to him. Christopher Flanders' self-appointed destiny is to mean God to elderly ladies of wealth on the brink
of death, just as certain carved rocks on the Easter Islands
meant God to the inhabitants. The magnificent, moribund
Flora Goforth, accustomed to having her every whim in-
stantly catered to, commands Chris: "Well, *bring* Him, I'm

ready to lay out a red carpet for Him, but how do you bring Him? Whistle? Ring a bell for Him?"[17] But this imperious attitude is more suitable for summoning a sacred cow on the streets of Bombay; and so when God, in the face of the fiercely ringing bell, remains silent, persevering in "the absolute speechlessness" imputed to Him by the Heckler, you cannot really blame Him.

In *The Gnädiges Fräulein,* a one-act play, God is a superannuated caretaker—long since pensioned off for his services to babies and drunks—for the title character. The zany, pathetic Fräulein, in this pop-art play, competes with Cockaloony birds for thrown-away fish at the Key West docks. The occupation is hazardous: her eyes are gouged out by the Cockaloonies who resent nonunion help. Still she perseveres and, though blind, miraculously manages to catch a fish on one occasion. "It just landed in my jaws like God had thrown it to me."[18] The play is not a sick joke: it implies that God, not without his own survival problems in a world that is frightfully out of joint, looks out as best he can—often little that it is—for those who endure against terrible odds.

Immanence is the common denominator in all these only ostensibly diverse views of God. The traditional belief in a transcendent being called God—a God beyond human experience who reveals himself to man—has no appeal to Williams' characters. Foreign to them is the orthodox commitment to the transcendent God made known in his Son, Jesus Christ. This heresy is the keystone of the recent prominent "death of God" theology. The "death of God" is certainly the most dramatic and provocative way of expressing God's displacement or effacement in our postmodern age. As early as 1802, the slogan was employed by Hegel. And at the end of the nineteenth century, Nietzsche embodied the cry, "God is dead," in a myth. "The God who beheld everything, and also man: that God had to die! Man cannot endure it that such a witness should live."[19] Despite this obituary notice, the phenomenon did not become a popular concern until the publication of Gabriel Vahanian's book, *The Death of God,* in 1961.

This mood—variously formulated as the absence, death, disappearance, eclipse, irrelevance, or silence of God—finds its most eloquent expression in modern literature. And Tennessee Williams is on the board of trustees of the "God is dead" school of literary writers. We have already seen how God is "experienced" by his characters. And even though breathed-into-life characters have a being of their own so that a playwright cannot be charged with believing everything they do and say, still the presumption here is that they do speak for their creator. For as Mrs. Venable remarks: "A poet's life is his work and his work is his life."[20] Besides, the frequency with which this radical immanentism turns up in Williams' dramas suggests that it represents his own belief and experience. It throbs with his sense of reality; it is far from a theatrical pose.

Williams' inability to grasp the possibility of the world being grounded in a transcendent Presence and his reliance on secular values as a source of moral action and religious belief probably explain, in part at least, why his literature is a literature of exhausted romanticism. By exhausted romanticism I mean the ambivalence of attraction and repulsion; the nexus of opposites, the convertibility of extremes; an upside-downness, an inside-outness—as well as other forms of inversion. This distorting mirror world of Williams exhibits the following traits: the Creator is equated with the lowliest of created things; innocence is equated with evil; life is equated with death; the soul is equated with the body.

The first characteristic of Williams' tired romanticism was implicit in the foregoing survey. God, the erstwhile creator of the world, is represented as having lapsed into degeneracy and impotency in *Camino Real.* God is seen as Joyce's aloof deity unconcernedly paring his fingernails in *Sweet Bird of Youth.* Williams' concept of God is deistic in these two plays. They represent his sole concession to a time-honored concept of God: God is where we come from and where we go, but he is not involved in the world in any meaningful way. In *Suddenly Last Summer, The Night of the Iguana,* and *Kingdom of Earth,* God is viewed as a composite of many destructive forces in nature and as indifferent to suffering. For example, the Rev. Shannon cuts the iguana loose with a machete "so it can run back to its bushes because God won't do it and we are going to play God here."[21] *The Milk Train Doesn't Stop Here Anymore* and *The Gnädiges Fräulein* modify the latter point by portraying God as a whimsical consoler: he withholds consolation from old ladies who are dying, but he bestows trifles upon victims of Cockaloony birds.

The second characteristic of Williams' tired romanticism is related to the first. If God is a passive, crotchety, irresponsible being, Christ fares no better: he is an object of derision. Williams has delineated four Christ figures: Val Xavier (*Orpheus Descending*), Chance Wayne (*Sweet Bird of Youth*), Reverend Shannon, and Christopher Flanders. All four are fallen, somewhat unlovely characters: prudish libertines with an air of nobility. These attractive vagabonds lead lives that display an ironic parallel with Christ's. Easter is the time setting for two of the plays. Val is burned alive on Holy Saturday; Chance is mutilated on Easter Sunday. The redemptive pattern of Easter is suggested in the transformation that the two undergo at the end of their respective plays. They both shun opportunities to escape from their tormentors and voluntarily submit to destruction for what they envision as a greater good. Shannon indulges himself in a voluptuous Passion Play performance: forcibly trussed up in a hammock, he twists and groans and imagines himself suffering for the guilt of the world. Christopher stars in an equally voluptuous temptation-of-Christ drama: he is tempted on a mountaintop by the Satanic Vera and made the target of a seduction by the neo-Magdalenic Flora. Vera promises to promote him as an artist and lay the wealth and social aristocracy of Capri at his feet; Flora taunts him with "Can you walk on water?"[22]

There is much more to show that Williams intended Val Xavier, Chance Wayne, the Rev. Shannon, and Chris Flanders to be pseudonyms of Christ, but full documentation of all the ironic parallels is beyond the scope of this chapter.

More important is the fact that Williams' vision of the *Christus* is unacceptable to most playgoers, not simply because there is too much narcissism, too much pagan Apollo in these impersonators; but this vision would make the gigolo, the world's most despicable professional lover, interchangeable with Christ, the world's most pure amateur lover.

The third characteristic of Williams' fatigued romanticism can be illustrated by Shannon's apotheosis of suicide. Shannon uses the threat of suicide—"the long swim to China"—as a means to power, as a way of controlling those around him. And he also deludes himself about it: he thinks of "the long swim to China" as another atonement, "another bit of voluptuous self-crucifixion."[23] His proposal to Hannah, concerning her 97-year-old poet-grandfather, Nonno, is another inversion of death and life. Shannon half seriously proposes a mercy killing to spare the old man the indignity of imminent eviction from a resort hotel to a seedy boardinghouse. At the same time, secure in the illusion that he is Christlike, he will use the occasion to aggrandize himself. "Put some hemlock in his poppyseed tea tonight . . . and I will consecrate it, turn it to God's blood. . . . I'll say, 'Take and drink this, the blood of our . . .' "[24] Christopher also finds in euthanasia the opportunity to celebrate the theme that life is found only in death. One day, swimming off a beach that he took to be deserted, he suddenly hears a cry from an old gentleman on the shore. "He called 'Help!' to me, as if he was in the water drowning, and I was on the shore." The supplicant begs Chris to help him get from life into death. Chris obliges, leading him out in the water. "Once he started to panic; I had to hold onto him tight as a lover till he got back his courage."[25] Chris, the Angel of Death, finds his vocation in giving people what he alleges they need: the notion that life is fulfilled in death; that death has greater dignity than life.

Desperately lonely people populate Williams' plays. Val speaks for most of them when he laments: "We're all of us locked up tight inside our bodies. Sentenced you might say to solitary confinement inside our own skins."[26] Parole is by way of sex: they regard sex as a means to salvation. They make love in order to interrupt loneliness. Some, like Blanche du Bois and Alma Winemiller, fail altogether to communicate with another human being: they stumble on *angst* and quail before the void. The sexual union, which they fastidiously mistake for a more encompassing one, destroys them. Some achieve rapport with another human being, but most of those who do, like Val and Chance, pay a terrifyingly high price for it. Sex leads to violent destruction and terrible punishment.

Still others, in order to overcome their guilt feelings about the act of copulation, fleck it with religious significance, and this leads to the fourth characteristic of Williams' fatigued romanticism. Shannon illustrates best this mixture of spiritual and carnal love. His behavior with complaisant young ladies takes one of two courses: either they begin with prayer and end up fornicating or vice versa—the reclining position turns to a kneeling position. In the one case, they pray for the strength to resist temptation; in the latter, they pray for forgiveness. In either case, the aftermath is the same: Shannon despises the lady almost as much as he despises himself. The "intimate connection," viewed by him as "the coupling of beasts,"[27] does little to stanch his loneliness. His enjoyment of a woman is slight, because he sees the body as corrupt; nonetheless, he pursues sensuality sadly and worships a sexy cross.

The "God is dead" slogan, so relentlessly dramatized by Williams, is actually sensational Protestant shorthand for "theology as traditionally conceived is dead." The old theology, bedrocked on the belief that God is transcendent, *beyond* being, perished at the end of the last century. The opposing notion, that God is immanent, *in* being, has become the keystone of the new theology. In a multiplicity of dazzling ways, the plays of Tennessee Williams reflect the prevailing theology.

That anything has been changed by the playwright's 1969 conversion to Roman Catholicism is a moot point. Neither the circumstances of his conversion nor the two plays that have appeared since clarify the issue. The priest who received him into the faith said that Williams was motivated by gratitude for recovery from a near-fatal illness. The priest also disputed press reports that had said the playwright "accepted everything in his profession of faith except immortality."[28] The initial post-conversion play, *In the Bar of a Tokyo Hotel* (1969), explores the decay of an artist, rather than the decay of God. And if you overlook the one brief allusion, at the outset of the chapter, associating masturbation with religion, God is also an absentee in the latest play, *Small Craft Warnings.* Genital experience, one half of the typical Williams' equation, is abundant in both; but God experience, the other half, is unexpectedly missing. It remains to be seen what will happen in future plays. Will the old theological dimension be restored? Will a new one replace it? Or will continued neglect prevail?

Up until very recently then, the quest for God, albeit a dying One, and the search for salvation through sex were Williams' most persistent concerns. The novels of Jean Genet are an inverted mirror image of the plays of Williams. The Frenchman's submoral oxymorons amount to a quest for Satan, an "evil God," and a search for damnation through sex. The duplicitous nature of these ignoble strivings is set down in the ensuing chapter.

5

Jean Genet

COUNTERFEIT SAINT

Jean Genet treats the passion of sexual perverts with the exaltation once reserved by canonized saints for the Passion of Christ. Perversion and crime are Genet's only subjects and no one else has ever written about them with such pretentiousness. He describes both as if they were states of grace. He manages to insinuate a kind of deranged poetry around the actions of homosexuals and murderers so as to invest them with a bizarre sacramentality. The Genet *oeuv* could be entitled The Imitation of Satan; the spiritual under world has found its Thomas à Kempis.

Genet's childhood was a disaster. Abandoned in the crad by his unwed mother and placed in a foundling home, I divided childhood and early youth between a foster hom and a reform school to which he was sentenced for the Later, until roughly the age of thirty, he was an itinera criminal. When not imprisoned, he prowled through the European underworld—Spain, his native France, Belgiur Poland, Czechoslovakia, and Nazi Germany—a beggar, thief, a traitor, a male prostitute. In *The Thief's Journal,* laments: "Everywhere it was the same: robbery, prison, ar from everyone of these countries, expulsion."[1]

To revenge himself upon a world that had rejected him, resolutely rejected it. Having been humiliated as a child the world, he would grow up to humiliate the world. The taunted child would survive to taunt society by outrageously flouting the approved code, by wallowing in every kind of depravity. Before society, he flings down the gauntlet: "The greater my guilt in your eyes, the more whole, the more totally assumed, the greater will be my freedom." Genet deliberately chooses to live "with my head bowed and in accordance with an ethic contrary to the one which governs the world." To implement this manifesto of defiance, designed, he alleges, to "perfect my solitude and uniqueness,"[2] he indulges in antisocial behavior galore. He befriends only those whom society despises, manipulates sin and filth for maximum shock value, worships failure, and practices metaphysical nihilism.

Genet is exhilarated by loving the one whom all others detest—the "scoundrel, blackguard, riffraff, guttersnipe, hoodlum, crook."[3] He glorifies every manner of criminal. In the *Miracle of the Rose,* he presents Harcamone, a child-rapist and murderer, as an august sacrificial figure around whom a prison community moves like the faithful around the figure of Christ during the Passion. All the machinery to turn the most perverted into the most godlike is present: Harcamone's proper milieu is the tabernacle; he arrives and departs "in sun and lightning"[4]; he is kissed by a celestial being; he bears a ladder on his shoulder and stumbles under the weight of it; he is tortured by the guards "even more when they sensed his power, but what would they have said had they learned of his miracles?" In addition, he quickens "an entire attentive people . . . with his supernatural perm,"[5] suffers "one of the greatest misfortunes in history,"[6] and holds out to the faithful the promise that they "will bear forever the sacred stigmata of the decapitation." Finally "the open grille in the door [of his cell] could be closed only by a small grate, like the *Judas* [my italics] holes in convents."[7]

Genet chooses the most despicable, most feared man in order to worship him as a god, luxuriating in the certainty that he is alone in recognizing the god's secret virtues. Harcamone, a repulsive brute, exudes sweetness and light nowhere except in Genet's idolatry. "The newspapers had

mired him in the epithets 'the killer,' 'the monster.' "[8] Even
Genet, in an unguarded moment, admits that "he [Harca-
mone] was as dull in free life as he was dazzling in prison."[9]
Genet is elated at being the only one who adores the de-
servedly defeated, the humiliated, the vanquished. Harcamone's ignominious death on the scaffold is his moment of
supreme glory. En route to the guillotine, he becomes so
huge as to fill the universe—reminiscent of Sunday in Chesterton's *The Man Who Was Thursday*—whereas the judge,
lawyer, chaplain, and executioner "shrank until they were no
bigger than four bedbugs."[10] They climb upon his person and
enter his interior via his ear and mouth. The interior exploration proceeds until they arrive at his heart where "a red rose
of monstrous size and beauty" is enshrined. They profane
"the Mystic Rose"[11]—a parody on Dante?—as a prelude to
beheading Harcamone.

The heroic virtues ascribed to Harcamone adorn other
criminals as well. The *Miracle of the Rose* ends on this note
of tribute: "Who, it will be asked, were Bulkaen, Harcamone,
Divers, who was Pilorge, who was Guy? And their names will
inspire awe, as we are awed by the light from a star that has
been dead a thousand years."[12] Genet celebrates the Mystical Body of Criminals. He is gripped by the mystery of Harcamone "who had been able to pursue the adventure of all
of us [criminals] to its most tenuous peak: the death on the
scaffold which is our glory."[13] And speaking of the great
lamentation that surged over the prison community at Harcamone's execution, he writes: "A mysterious thread of kinship, a delicate affinity, unites the criminals of the whole
world, and they are all affected when something happens to
one of them."[14]

Our Lady of the Flowers, who at the age of sixteen stran-
gled an old man gratuitously, is another executed murderer
whose trial alone haloed him as the saints of the church are
haloed. In the courtroom, all the spectators "could read,
graven in the aura of Our Lady of the Flowers, the following
words: 'I am the Immaculate Conception.' "[15] The prosecut-
ing attorney is nervous lest he say or do something that

"would transform him into the devil's advocate and would justify canonization of the murderer."[16] During the cross-examination, Our Lady becomes another inverted Christ figure: he "was as prodigiously glorious as the body of Christ rising aloft, to dwell there alone and fixed, in the sunny noonday sky."[17] After the death sentence is pronounced and Our Lady is given back to the guards, "he seemed to them invested with a sacred character, like the kind that expiatory victims, whether goat, ox, or child, had in olden times. . . . The guards spoke to him and served him as if, knowing he was laden with the weight of the sins of the world, they had wanted to bring down upon themselves the benediction of the Redeemer."[18] Genet's compulsion is not simply to "Christify" the murderer in his own right but rather to impute this inversion of values, where the most shameful becomes the most noble, to society at large and, ironically, especially to the court officers and crowd.

This blasphemous apotheosis of the gratuitous homicide is coupled with pornography and scatology in order to *épater le bourgeois*. When his sinful actions did not sufficiently horrify society, Genet turned to sinful words. What he could not accomplish by his thefts, his perversions, his betrayals, he would achieve with his audacious long-suppressed pornography. He makes his readers, those of us whose world is rectitude, pay for the indignities we heaped upon him by making us taste with loathing our own unsuspected wickedness. He catches us up in the coils of slimiest sin, if only vicariously. He forces us to think disquieting thoughts and harbor doubts. And even when his sick romanticism finally repels us with its topsy-turviness—like the Marquis de Sade, he makes vice a virtue and pain a pleasure—he lavishes so much artistry on it that we still begrudgingly admire, even though we do not approve. For example, homosexuality, in every squalid detail, is made to appear superior to heterosexuality. "Hard muscles and harmonious faces were meant to sing and glorify the odious functions of my friends and to impose them upon you."[19] Homosexual outcasts are invariably handsome and dazzling, and homosexuality is paradoxically more virile than heterosexuality. Remark Darling's proud cry: "A male that fucks another male is a double male!"[20]

According to legend, when Satan is feeling amorous he purchases the solace of young women whom he covets. But after the amour, he plays a prank: the jewels turn into excrement. The same holds for Genet who contends that one of the highest expressions of beauty is excrement. Enthusiastically, he relates how he accustomed himself to excrement—he served an apprenticeship on farts—how he found scatophagy appealing, and how he allowed himself "to drift into this so readily because in that way I estrange myself from the world. I am carried along in that fall which, cutting by its very speed and verticality all threads that hold me to the world, plunges me into prison, into foulness, into dreaming and hell, and finally lands me in a garden of saintliness where roses bloom, roses whose beauty—as I shall know then—is composed of the rims of the petals, their folds, gashes, tips, spots, insect holes, blushes, and even their stems which are mossy with thorns."[21] Genet, fascinated as well as repulsed by feces, accomplishes two purposes here. By exalting human waste matter, he alienates the middle class. But more than that, by coating excrement with the scent of roses, he reveals himself to be a practical joker on the order of Satan: he uses ephemeral beauty—beauty that is evolving into ordure—to have his way with others and to humiliate them. "My art," Genet says to the middle class with characteristic bluntness, "is the art of making you eat shit."[22] His tongue-in-cheek goal is to convert us to scatophagy; his actual aim is to persuade us what it feels like to be utterly debased. This yields him the satisfaction of knowing that he has made us deeply uncomfortable.

Ostensibly Genet lives to defeat himself. Failure appears to be the goal of his life. He seems indifferent to the stakes that other men play for, victory and success. "If I cannot have the most brilliant destiny, I want the most wretched."[23] To this infantile admission, there is an unuttered corollary: "If I cannot have the most brilliant woman, I want the most wretched man." He boldly courts catastrophe. "I accumulate rash acts:

getting into stolen cars, walking in front of stores where I have operated, showing obviously fake papers. . . . But while I hope for misfortune as an act of grace . . . I want to fulfill myself in the rarest of destinies." The qualification introduces ambivalence. By breaking everything wide open, he has it both ways: he appeases society, for he appears to be overcome; but at the same time he defies that same society, for he sees himself as overcoming. Abjection is despair, but "despair was strength itself."[24] If he is vanquished by the sordidness of his life, he triumphs as a man of letters. "Grief and despair are possible only if there is a way out, whether visible or secret."[25] The art that snatches success from failure and turns the tables on society is his secret way out.

Ceres, offended by Erysichthon, punished him with an insatiable appetite. In the end, Erysichthon ate himself. Genet, too, would practice autocannibalism. "I wanted to swallow myself, by opening my mouth very wide and turning it over my head so that it would take in my whole body, and then the Universe."[26] But his consumption potential is so much more ambitious: it makes Erysichthon's punishment puny by comparison. Genet is not content to devour himself, even to devour mankind; he would devour God. The manner of consumption is not original: it parodies the practice of the faithful at Holy Communion. "It was within me that I established this divinity. . . . I swallowed it."[27] This gastric conquest of God led to Genet's Nietzschean desire to impersonate him, perhaps even to replace him. "As I grow strong, I am my own god. I dictate."[28] And lest there be any doubt, in *Funeral Rites,* he boasts: "I was sure that I was the god. I was God."[29] There was a childhood sacrilege—real or fancied —that first made him bold in the Divine Presence. *Our Lady of the Flowers* relates how little Culafroy (Genet himself) stole up to the altar in an empty church and secretly profaned the Host. The trembling boy expected God to appear and to sentence him to eternal damnation. When nothing happened, when the sacrilege went unpunished, the child lost faith, and the incident became the first in a series of profanations. For a long time, Genet habitually received communion in a state of mortal sin, mentally cursing the Host as he chewed it; all the time thinking "that the idea of God is something I harbor in my bowels."[30] He is without pristine gestures: he is the opposite of Stephen the deacon, for instance, who swallowed the Host to *save* it from profanation. Genet has a passion for desecration. "I desired only to commit a sacrilege, to soil the purity of a family."[31]

Throughout his books, the god of Genet is Genet himself, and since the aspect of God the Father that appeals to him most is the unique infinite creativity, Genet likes to present himself as the creator of the universe. Unlike G. M. Hopkins' poetical world where everything "is charged with the grandeur of God," everything in Genet's fictive world fathers him forth—"It is the universe for which I am meant. It is meant for me"[32]—in a pseudo-pantheistic way. Watching the sun rise, from the rocks overlooking Porto Reale, he fantasies: "It was within my body that it rose, continued its curve and completed it. If I saw it in the sky of the astronomers, I did so because it was the bold projection there of the one I preserved within myself."[33] Genet becomes a creator *manqué* who reverses divine creation by making himself the sole object of the creation. "I would have liked a visible, dazzling glory to be manifest at my fingertips, would have liked my potency to lift me from the earth, to explode within me and dissolve me, to shower me to the four winds. I would have rained over the world. My powder, my pollen, would have touched the stars."[34] Here he identifies himself with, makes himself over into, some overwhelming, rhetorical, melodramatic force of nature. To that extent, he reflects a kind of literature that was very popular from 1820 to 1840, especially with Byron, who created it, and Shelley. But Genet goes beyond this nineteenth-century Romantic tradition: he is not merely raining for his readers. The dangerous desire to be the demiurge grows in his mind like the pressure of an orgasm. He equates a sense of power with sex.

This narcissism, mounted on a macrocosmic scale—so that Genet is everything and everything is Genet—is further evident in these lines in which Genet speaks of himself in the third person: "Swallows nest beneath his arms. They have masoned a nest there of dry earth. Snuff-colored velvet caterpillars mingle with the curls of his hair. Beneath his feet, a hive of bees, and broods of asps behind his eyes."[35] Solipsism reinforces narcissism: "When I tell one of them [prisoners] that I love him, I wonder whether I am not telling it to myself. . . . I mean that the solitude of prison gave me the freedom to be with the hundred Jean Genets glimpsed in a hundred passers-by."[36] Megalomania reinforces solipsism: "The world dwindled, and its mystery too, as soon as I was cut off from it."[37] He has nothing to say about nature, or about other people, or indeed about anything except himself. In his lonely prison cell, in his imaginary realm, Genet converts his impotence into omnipotence by forcing the real world to withdraw, "until it is only a golden point in . . . a somber sky,"[38] so that he may impersonate God in reverse and change multiplicity into the oneness of himself.

Unlike most other creative writers who think of themselves as creators after the Creator, Genet deludes himself into thinking that he is creating the universe from scratch. His aspiration is to be the sole character in a drama modeled on the book of Genesis. "Heroized, my book [*The Thief's Journal*], which has become my Genesis, contains . . . the commandments which I cannot transgress. . . . To what shall I refer if not to it?"[39] He practices belles-lettres in order to be supremely self-sufficient, but he is not without anxieties, unbecoming a self-appointed deity. He fears that "I shall lose the grace that has enabled me to seek news of heaven."[40]

Genet seeks the "news of heaven" best in *The Thief's Journal*—the book that Sartre calls "the most beautiful that Genet has written, the *Dichtung und Wahrheit* of homosexuality."[41] In "heaven" Genet learned that "there is a close relationship between flowers and convicts," for one thing. "Should I have to portray a convict—or a criminal—" he continues, "I shall so bedeck him with flowers that, as he disappears beneath them, he will himself become a flower, a gigantic and new one."[42] This metamorphosis occurs throughout his work. Harcamone becomes a rose: "Har-

camone appeared before a warden who was dismayed at
being confronted with a mystery as absurd as that of a rose
in full bloom."⁴³ When Darling, the pimp, has his eyes black-
ened by fists, they promptly become "two bouquets of vio-
lets."⁴⁴ Homosexual revels become flower festivals: Roger, a
minor character in *The Thief's Journal,* in the course of a
seduction, plants red carnations among his toes, between his
buttocks, in his mouth, and under his armpits. By investing
convicts with the glamour of flowers, Genet robs flowers of
their lofty connotation: he steals fragrance from a noble
word. Flowers are reduced to the criminal's colophon—jail-
bird flora. By the same token, the criminals who are transformed into flowers are also reduced: they are ultimately
swallowed up by the flower like an insect caught in a Venus's-
flytrap. Genet's passion for flowers takes a variety of forms:
he fills his room with them; he covers acquaintances, living
and dead, with them; and he features them in book titles. All
this recalls Ronald Firbank, who was joined to flowers in
exactly the same ways, with the difference that he had trouble paying his florist's bills. Genet has no such problem: he
usually steals flowers, mostly from cemeteries.

In *Our Lady of the Flowers,* Genet admits his compulsion
to diminish reality. "But the fact is that my longing for a
splendid imaginary destiny has, as it were, condensed the
tragic, purple elements of my actual life into a kind of extremely compact, solid, and scintillating reduction."⁴⁵ In his
nearly exhaustive evaluation, *Saint Genet,* Sartre summa-
rizes Genet's hang-up brilliantly. "Genet's creation is the
reverse of divine creation . . . whereas the divine creation is
a procession which goes from nonbeing to the infinite multiplicity of being, that of Genet is a recession which draws
indefinitely nearer and nearer to nothingness without ever
quite reaching it. . . . He is relieving the world of its matter
as a pickpocket relieves a victim of his wallet."⁴⁶ Most creative writers wish to *add* being to the world; Genet desires to
subtract being from the world.

Having robbed men of their substance, Genet promptly
appropriates it. Whatever the individuality of his characters,

there always comes a time when he absorbs them into himself. While insisting on Harcamone's extramental existence, he informs us nonetheless that ultimately Harcamone's "adventure transpired . . . in the highest region of myself."[47] The fact that at bottom all his characters are himself is best illustrated in *Our Lady of the Flowers.* "From myself I make Divine," sex: male; predilection: female; compulsion: transvestism. "Is it I or Divine who will receive him [Darling, Divine's lover]?" And "when I tell one of them that I love him, I wonder whether I am not telling it to myself."[48] Like that of the tortured poet, Artaud, Genet's self-absorption finally becomes tedious and for the same reason: it is a kind of endless linguistic onanism which often collapses into obscene blasphemy. That is the case here. This is black transubstantiation. After bread and wine are changed into the body and blood of Christ, Christ inhabits others, installing himself in the faithful when he is received at Holy Communion; after other people are changed into Genet, they inhabit him, being installed against their will in a diabolical host. By a monstrously appetitive love, he manages to swallow all his personae. The activity of mourning in *Funeral Rites,* a eulogy to Jean Decarnin, Genet's twenty-year-old lover and member of the underground who was shot down during the street fighting accompanying the liberation of Paris in 1944, is cannibalistic. By reveling in the fantasy of eating Decarnin's corpse, Genet not only swallows the glorified body of his lover as if it were a host, but he excites himself into an empathic identification with Decarnin's collaborationist slayers, which obviously facilitates his necrophagia.

The situation is always the same in all of Genet's sexual fantasies: the homoerotic relationship terminates with the destruction—usually the death—of his partner. At the end of the *Miracle of the Rose,* Bulkaen is shot down in an aborted attempt to escape from prison, and Harcamone is beheaded. In *Our Lady of the Flowers,* Genet reigns in solitary splendor after the deaths of Divine and Our Lady and the imprisonment of Darling. Two factors stand out here. Genet is capable of experiencing other human beings only through manipulation and total control of them. This explains his adoration of Hitler. And Genet's impulse to love men—apparently he never had the desire to love a woman—is inseparable from the impulse to murder them.

Frequently, as an encore to lovemaking, the female scorpion devours her male. Genet is a close student of the insect world. He has learned how to consume his innumerable mates: he shrinks them by so-called passive homosexuality. He prefers to be the party who plays the woman's role. What he says of one cohort applies to almost all: "In order to *tame* [italics added] him, I allowed him to have the superiority of the male over me."[49] Castration, by way of fellatio and buggery, is the method employed by Genet "in order to tame" his consorts. Coitus so conceived amounts to the systematically pursued death of the "male," whom the "female" unconsciously despises. Genet chooses lovers who possess the qualities he envies, and he uses sex as a weapon to steal them. His desire for Stilitano, for example, is the desire to be cruel and handsome. To bring this off, Genet encourages the virile-looking Stilitano to take him, so that "he would fill out my muscles, loosen my gait, thicken my gestures. . . . Thus possessed, I knew I was capable of every kind of cruelty. . . . Instead of causing fright, my transformation adorned me with manly graces." When he observes that he is using his lover's gestures, words, and even seminal fluid "the way one touches relics whose magic is urgently needed,"[50] he displays an atavistic attitude toward semen—which he apostrophizes as "the racing pulsation of the sperm"[51]—and implicitly a fetishistic attitude toward cannibalism. To return to the original metaphor: Genet is the scorpion who devours her male in order to re-create him inside herself with her own substance in her own image and likeness. "I . . . knew that Stilitano was my own creation and that its destruction depended upon me."[52] Despite all the grandiose phraseology he expends on his lovemaking, Genet's love is only the lofty name which he gives to masturbation. He masturbates his partners to draw their strength into himself.

Religious imagery accompanies this hostile perversion of

the sexual act. The "man" in a homosexual couple, at the moment of orgasm, is limned as godlike. Whenever Divine, a male prostitute, is penetrated by "her" pimp, Darling, "her" body would cry out: 'The god, behold the god!' "[53] Thus Darling earns the following salutation: "The Eternal passed by in the form of a pimp."[54] There is also something of Lawrentian penis worship in these sodomistic relationships: concurring with D. H. Lawrence, Genet locates the soul in the crotch. He defines the soul as "that which emerges . . . from the member."[55] The penis that enters him is at once divine, the seat of the soul, and a relic. "Behind Stilitano's fly it was the sacred Black Stone to which Heliogabalus offered up his imperial wealth."[56] As such it deserves adoration. The homage that Genet pays is of three kinds. Sometimes he fervently fashions phallic epithets: "such expressions as Little Dicky, the Babe in the Cradle, Jesus in His Manger, the Hot Little Chap, your Baby Brother. . . ."[57] Just as fervently, he sometimes celebrates phallic cults, replete with feathers, flowers, and ribbons, "behind the curtain of buttoned flies."[58] And sometimes with equal ardor, he composes phallic litanies: "Oh my solid, oh my fierce, oh my burning one! Oh my Bees [prison argot for abbey] watch over us!"[59]

In describing homosexuals and homosexual intercourse, Genet then frequently has recourse to impiety and blasphemy. Like the hysterical Rimbaud, he cultivates a nexus between the unnatural and the supernatural. The Holy Family is sometimes the model evoked for a homosexual tableau *vivant*, as in the following: "We [two adolescent boys] pulled the woolen blankets over our heads, and for a moment we lay still, as in the cradles where Byzantine painters often confine the Virgin and Child. . . ."[60] Irreverence is usually aimed at either God the Father or Christ. The ascension of Jesus is twice mocked in *Our Lady*. "Darling went up the stairs two at a time, an ample and forthright ascension, which may lead, after the roof, on steps of blue air, up to heaven."[61] Divine, too, is extended this unique privilege. God is so smitten with "her saintliness" that he aspires to lift her bodily up to heaven. But determined "to cling to earth

and not rise to heaven,"[62] Divine successfully struggles
against him. She does not reciprocate his affection, and, besides, she has positive contempt for the second Person of the
blessed Trinity. Undressed, one evening, "she saw with fresh
eyes her white, hairless body, smooth and dry, and, in places,
bony. She was ashamed of it and hastened to put out the
lamp, for it was the ivory body of Jesus on an eighteenth-
century crucifix, and relations with the divinity, even a
resemblance to it, sickened her."[63] Nonetheless, Divine finds
the resemblance flattering, for when she has fainted, after
being arrested for hustling in drag, and the policemen stand
over her fanning her with their handkerchiefs, she proudly
proclaims: "They were the Holy Women wiping my face. My
Divine Face."[64] In her hierarchy of values, homosexual love
is all. "Divine made of her loves a god above God, Jesus, and
the Holy Virgin, to whom they were submissive like everyone else."[65]

Often it is the Mass, the altar, and the church that are
associated with homosexuality. Genet is in the Black Mass
tradition. Divine, who worships Darling, says, "When I see
him lying naked, I feel like saying mass on his chest."[66] The
offertory, the most sacred part of the Mass, provides Genet
with the opportunity to give the greatest offense. "Behold,
my darlings, behold Divine wedded to God. She rises at
cock's crow to go to communion, the Quite-Repentant."[67] By
means of a pun, he insinuates a blasphemous parallel between fellatio and Holy Communion. And when Divine
shows a small photo of Our Lady to Mimosa, another "femi-
nine" homosexual, "she" puts it on her tongue and swallows
it, "the way one swallows the Eucharist."[68] In describing
Decarnin, Genet declares that "these lines are the key that
opens the tabernacle and reveals the Host."[69] In his black
looking-glass world, it is only the impure in heart who are
Christlike. Again he confuses the tabernacle with a male
brothel. "It [a homosexual love nest] is the infinitely precious
tabernacle where the witness keeps vigil."[70] Even the sacramentals are not exempt. Of Stilitano, he observes: His "poste-
rior was a Station [of the cross]."[71]

To illustrate adequately, let alone fully, the degree to which Genet has recourse to religious images whenever he refers to homosexuality would require a long essay unto itself. I have presented only a small fraction of the evidence; yet, I hope, enough to suggest that he is almost a prisoner of verbal automatism. Why? The explanation that he gives is disappointing. "Excited in my random readings by coming upon terms evoking religiosity, I quite naturally made use of them in musing on my loves, which by being so named took on monstrous proportions. . . . Perhaps love, the better to create me, acquainted me with those elements which summon forth the heady words that are used to name them: cults, ceremonials, visitations, litanies, royalty, magic. . . ."[72] By using a theological vocabulary to muse on his loves, he tries to accomplish a twofold purpose. By coupling sacrilege and pornography, his work takes "on monstrous proportions" in the eyes of the bourgeois reader. Another motive, and one somewhat at variance with the first, is his own largely unconscious desire to hide from himself the necessarily sterile nature of this relationship that Lord Alfred Douglas, Wilde's catamite, once characterized as "the love that dare not speak its name."[73] (Now, of course, it is the love that ceases not to speak its name.)

But the underlying motive for this compulsive association of homosexuality with religion has cosmic masturbatory overtones. Genet employs this religion-ridden erotic mythology, because it enables him to consummate his ultimate ambition—to "jerk off" the world. "It was a good thing that I raised egoistic masturbation to the dignity of a cult. I have only to begin the gesture and a kind of unclean and supernatural transposition displaces the truth. . . . The external vision of the props of my desire isolates me far from the world."[74] This text from *Our Lady* finds its exemplum in *Funeral Rites*. After Jean Decarnin, a Resistance hero and secret homosexual, is slain, Genet, in defiance of the public ceremony, privately memorializes him by stroking a matchbox that he carries in his pocket. The matchbox becomes the deceased's mini-coffin, the pocket a cathedral, and Genet a priest presiding over a Black Requiem Mass. "I was performing in my pocket, on the box that my hand was stroking, a diminutive funeral ceremony."[75] A series of transformations occurs: the world is transformed into a matchbox; the matchbox into Decarnin's corpse which is then transformed into Genet's penis. *Funeral Rites* is the supreme epic of masturbation: a fantasy that should shame Portnoy all the way to Sweden for an organ transplant.

Genet rings a variation on Descartes: I do evil. Therefore I am. In other words, he makes evil a religious imperative in order to affirm his existence. He solemnly apostrophizes Satanism: "Evil, wonderful evil, you who remain when all goes to pot, miraculous evil, you're going to help us. I beg you, evil . . . impregnate my people."[76] Moreover, the evil he identifies with is beautiful. "The beauty of a moral act depends on the beauty of its expression. The act is beautiful if it provokes, and in our throat reveals, song. . . . This means that treachery is beautiful if it makes us sing."[77] From the most heinous act, a felicitous power of expression is able to extract beauty. Treachery in the grand style, executed with lyrical grace, can be beautiful. By implication, lack of style will render the most sublime act ugly. Fidelity to a noble cause, performed without imagination, can be ugly. The execution of an act is all important; the substance is of little consequence. Ethics is trimmed to fit aesthetics. Genet insists that "the fulfillment of my legend consists of the boldest possible criminal existence," because he believes that the bold are beautiful. His rare destiny, with "a hitherto unseen beauty, beautiful because of the danger which works away at it, overwhelms it, undermines it,"[78] is hilt evil. The evil he zeroes in on is intended not merely to destroy himself but the world as well. "I wish for a moment to focus attention on the reality of supreme happiness in despair: when one is suddenly alone, confronting one's sudden ruin, when one witnesses the irremediable destruction of one's work and self. I would give all the wealth of this world—indeed it must be given—to experience the desperate—and secret—state which no one knows I know. Hitler, alone, in the cellar of his palace, during the last minutes of the defeat of Germany, surely experienced that moment of pure light—fragile and solid lucidity—the awareness of his fall."[79] Because of this worship of evil he has been compared to Baudelaire but more exact is the similarity to Hitler, whom he cannot help envying—the greater the fall, the greater the glory.

Genet's proximate goal is the ecstasy of annihilation; his ultimate goal in sacrificing the world and himself is to gain entree to the kingdom of darkness. This despite the fact that, unlike Anatole France, he does not uniquely contend that the legions of Lucifer defeated the hosts of heaven in the primordial war. Begrudgingly he admits that "God is the final victor."[80] But with characteristic consistency he opts for the losing side—this time the quintessence of loss. However, he is still *quasi*-Manichaean, for, like Milton, he makes Satan the more charismatic of the two eternal adversaries. This accounts for his whim that the devil has the superior personnel. Genet fancies that only the brave and handsome are recruited for the ministry of evil. All Nazi soldiers, for instance, are endowed with courage and good looks. And manly grace is nowhere so evident as in his gallery of pimps —those "handsome thugs that charm" him with " 'the black light . . . the blazing shade . . .' "—who represent "the living . . . synthesis of Evil and the Beautiful."[81] The minions of the Prince of Darkness do not rely on greater physical beauty exclusively; they possess another advantage as well. "Only intelligent people are capable of understanding evil—and hence the only ones capable of committing it,"[82] Genet proclaims.

It comes as a surprise to discover that Genet aspires to sanctity. "Unable to give a definition of saintliness," he relates that nevertheless "I want at every moment to create it, that is, to act so that everything I do may lead me to it . . . until I am so luminous that people will say 'He is a saint.' " Inasmuch as sanctity, conventionally understood, is the pursuit of moral perfection, this manifesto might be construed as a maxi-put-on. But that is not the case. Genet was never more serious: without this quest his life would be vain.

"I wish to be a saint chiefly because the word indicates the loftiest human attitude, and I shall do everything to succeed." The so-called saintliness that he quests for has few features in common with sanctity conventionally understood. In fact, removing the Christian meaning from saintliness is scarcely a lesser goal than practicing his unique concept of the word. What he objects to in the Christian practice —the insistence on moral perfection—is precisely what he himself is most deficient in and has the greatest contempt for. Whenever his id and his conscience are in conflict, he always shakes off the counsel of the latter. "Starting from the elementary principles of morality and religion, the saint arrives at his goal if he sheds them."[83] His authority is the Biblical text " 'Taking upon Himself the sins of the world,' " which he interprets literally. It "means exactly this: experiencing . . . in their effects all sins; it means having subscribed to evil."[84] This constitutes Genet's indictment of the canonized saint: he is unwilling to subscribe to evil, to let sin swish around in his bloodstream. "I distrust the saintliness of Vincent de Paul. He should have been willing to commit the galley slave's crime instead of merely taking his place in irons."[85]

"Saintliness means turning pain to good account. It means forcing the devil to be God. It means obtaining the recognition of evil."[86] A brief examination of each of the three conditions that Genet assigns to saintliness will fix his many dissimilarities as well as his few similarities to the canonized saint. In *The Journal,* where he discusses the subject at greater length and more explicitly than elsewhere, he declares: "It seems to me that its [saintliness'] sole basis is renunciation. . . . I shall use my pride and sacrifice it therein."[87] He does renounce pride but not in the manner of the Christian saint. Humility exalts the latter's behavior; humiliation degrades Genet's. He feels deeply grateful to the riffraff who permit him to be their sexual slave. Nor does he turn sacrifice to the same account as the Christian saint. "I make of sacrifice . . . the highest virtue. . . . There must be damnation in it."[88] Genet is a saint in reverse: he deliberately chooses to debase himself, to live with his head bowed, and to pursue his destiny toward darkness, in a direction opposite to his rival. If Sartre dubs Genet a saint, he is only following Genet, who affirms his search for saintliness "by way of sin." But this remains an inversion of the word's definition. I prefer to call him a counterfeit saint.

But, of course, the counterfeit imitates the genuine just enough to deceive. Like the canonized saint, Genet takes the devil for granted: he never doubts his existence. Unlike the other, Genet is sorely tempted to invoke Satan's power: he stops just short of praying to him. He flinches from making a compact with him—this "would be to commit oneself too deeply"[89]—but he constantly exploits the spell of the nether powers. Like the canonized saint, Genet practices self-mortification—he once wore next to his skin a clinging hair shirt —but unlike him, Genet's worldly detachment is evil-oriented. "Evil, like good, is attained gradually by means of an inspired insight . . . by daily, careful, slow, disappointing labor."[90] Elsewhere, however, with obvious but unacknowledged indebtedness to Nietzsche, Genet refers to himself as one of those who is laboring to give birth to a new morality "beyond good and evil, there where the saint must live."[91] He wavers between the two, and he never really resolves the dilemma—doing evil and launching himself beyond good and evil. Theoretically, at least, he prefers the latter. His ideal is "to commit a crime in order to free oneself from the yoke of the moral powers."[92] In the service of this ideal, he pays tribute to murder, theft, and treachery so motivated.

Genet's recurrent fantasy is to murder a handsome boy. He fulfills the dream by proxy: as we have seen in *Funeral Rites*, after his youthful lover is murdered by pro-Nazis, Genet profanes the corpse by deliberately submitting himself to the murderers. His fictive alter egos fulfill the wish literally: Erik, a German soldier, Harcamone, and Divine slay children. Erik commits premeditated murder—his victim is a handsome fifteen-year-old boy, unknown to him, who does nothing to provoke him—to attain "the highest moment of freedom. . . . To fire on God, to wound him and make him a deadly enemy."[93] Harcamone rapes and strangles a nine-year-old girl to veer close to death and to attain "purity." "The reason is that blood purifies, that it raises the one who sheds it to unwonted heights."[94] Standing on the pavement below, Divine looks up and entices a two-year-old out on to an insufficiently protected balcony. When the baby falls into the void, "none of the child's pirouettes was lost on her. She was superhuman, to the point of—without tears or cries or shudders—gathering with her gloved fingers what remained of the child." Divine performs "this inexpiable crime"[95] to ensure the death of goodness.

These grisly, infamous acts, performed by pederasts, fill Genet with joy, a joy he hastens to add that "should not be confused with sadism"; because his pleasure in them is "caused by the simple rightness of the audacity which dared, by massacring the delicate flesh of adolescents, to destroy a visible, established beauty in order to achieve a beauty—or poetry—resulting from that shattered beauty's encounter with that barbaric gesture."[96] Evil creates new, perhaps even greater, beauty, and "murder is the symbolic act of evil."[97] He longs for complicity in murder. "I would like to take upon myself Harcamone's act of murder,"[98] to bask in the reflected glory. In his effort to persuade the reader that murder can be beautiful, Genet unintentionally lapses into absurdities. He depicts unrestrained mass enthusiasm for this kind of ideological murderer—of whom Raskolnikov is the prototype. In the courtroom during the trial of Our Lady of the Flowers, who has achieved the kind of freedom that Genet prizes by garroting a harmless old man, a strange empathy prevails: "The crowd was ashamed of not being the murderer. . . . The crowd was ashamed of not dying. The religion of the hour was to . . . envy a young murderer."[99] Genet's black comedy becomes black magic with the irony intact. Our Lady who has convinced himself that he killed out of love of the beautiful succeeds in convincing everyone else except the one segment of society capable of punishing him —the law. The sober-miened law, alone able to withstand his infectious enthusiasm, decapitates him.

Theft and treachery undertaken to prove the superiority of the thief and the traitor are similarly lauded. Jimmying a door or picking a lock—"These are rites," Genet declares, "whose essence is still mysterious to me. . . . I was the young sovereign who takes possession of a new realm. . . . I was saved from bondage and low inclinations, for I had just performed an act of physical boldness. . . . I was now a man, a he-man."[100] Burglaries performed "in accordance with the rites"[101] purify the burglar. "I went to theft as to a liberation, to the light. I freed myself from prostitution and begging, the abjectness of which becomes increasingly apparent the more I am drawn by the glory of the theft."[102] Betrayal is also a rite of passage that draws him by its "glory." "I had the admirable courage," he asserts—without a trace of irony—"to turn my most tormented friend over to the police. . . . And I made a point of being paid off for my betrayal before his very eyes."[103]

Betrayal is the transcendent evil, since the betrayer is "established . . . in an indestructible solitude." Characteristically this is the state of being that Genet covets most. "It is perhaps their moral solitude—to which I aspire that makes me admire traitors and love them."[104] He defines at length the nature of this aspiration in *Funeral Rites.* "Having chosen to remain outside a social and moral world whose code of honor seemed to me to require . . . the precepts taught in school, it was by raising to the level of virtue . . . the opposite of the common virtues that I thought I could attain a moral solitude where I would never be joined. I chose to be a traitor, thief, looter, informer, hater, destroyer, despiser, coward. With ax and cries I cut the bonds that held me to the world of customary morality."[105] He divulges here the blueprint that has enabled him, as he sees it, to raise his life to the level of a saint and martyr; he stresses what he considers to be the ascetic nature of his choice freely made and argues for a notion that might be labeled sin mysticism, were he more orthodox. But since Genet's rhetoric is always more impressive than his logic, he is singularly lacking in persuasiveness. His vaunted free choice, resulting in self-conferred sanctity and martyr-

dom, manifests his unrivaled capacity for rationalization: so-
called free choice is actually the good face he puts upon his
compulsive, insatiable need to fumble toward an absolute in
abjection, betrayal, and submission. His contention that he
raises treachery, theft, looting, informing, hating, destroying,
despising, and cowardice "to the level of virtue" is more
upside-down semantics—the ultimate point of inverted
romanticism. And the implication that the deviant subcul-
ture he frequents, after he separates himself absolutely from
"the world of customary morality," is somehow a more exalted state is the greatest self-deception of all. Joseph Conrad
knew better. Conrad's indictment, in *Under Western Eyes*,
might serve as this *poète-maudit's* future epitaph: "No human being could bear a steady view of moral solitude without
going mad."[106]

For Genet the world is a male brothel. For Nathanael West
and Flannery O'Connor the world was a spiritual amusement
park. We next explore the Coney Island of the soul.

6

Wrestlers with Christ and Cupid

The trademark of Nathanael West and Flannery O'Connor is religious fanaticism coupled with sex. There is a close connection between getting high on Christ and sexual inhibition, sometimes perversion, in the work of both writers. West, the unbeliever obsessed with the search for belief, wrote about sophisticated Jesus freaks and gang-bang nightmares; O'Connor, the believer who mocked the notion that Christ "doesn't matter," wrote about Bible Belt Jesus freaks and satanic sodomists. In varying ways, their concerns are theological, or antitheological, as well as erotic.

1

Nathanael West, born Nathan Weinstein in New York City, received little or no education in the Jewish religion, suffered over his Jewishness, and was ashamed of it. At Brown University, he approached God artistically and mystically—"Latin poetry, medieval painting, Huysmans, stained-glass windows."[1] That the mysticism was unorthodox may be seen by the reference to Huysmans. Traditional mysticism, West associated with sexual repression: he conceived of Jesus and Mary and many canonized saints as antisexual figures. He was obsessed with the paradoxical Wagnerian theme of death through love.

In *Miss Lonelyhearts* (1933), West depicts two Christ-intoxicated men: Miss Lonelyhearts, pseudonym of an otherwise nameless man who does an advice-to-the-afflicted column for a New York newspaper; and William Shrike, the inhumane feature editor. Divine intoxication affects them very differently. Miss Lonelyhearts imbibes God to some advantage: it turns him into one of "the priests of twentieth-century America,"[2] singularly devoted to trying to alleviate the anguish of desperate correspondents. William Shrike is turned off by God-guzzling: he deliberately resists the suffusing warmth, becomes hateful, a self-hater, and mocks human misery. The novel opens with a venomous litany:

> Soul of Miss L, glorify me.
> Body of Miss L, nourish me.
> Blood of Miss L, intoxicate me.
> Tears of Miss L, wash me.
> Oh good Miss L, excuse my plea,
> And hide me in your heart,
> And defend me from mine enemies.
> Help me, Miss L, help me, help me.
> In *saecula saeculorum.* Amen.

With mocking devotion, Shrike preaches the gospel of Miss Lonelyhearts. "Christ," the malicious Shrike intones, is "the Miss Lonelyhearts of Miss Lonelyhearts."[3] This articulate antievangelist, with the marvelously apt name, is so misanthropic that he salivates cyanide and spritzs with a tongue flick.

Miss L. suffers from what he calls his "Christ complex,"[4] a complex with passionate appeal. "For him, Christ was the most natural of excitements."[5] But when he nails an ivory Christ, "removed . . . from the cross to which it had been fastened," to the wall of his room with great spikes and great expectations, it disappoints him: "Instead of writhing [like a snake] the Christ remained calmly decorative."[6] This Freudian Christ imagery is persistent. Crossing a park, "he walked into the shadow of a lamppost that . . . pierced him like a spear."[7] Observing the parched earth in the park, he resolves to beseech his petitioners "to come . . . and water the soil with their tears." He imagines Shrike advising him to teach them to pray: " 'Give us this day our daily stone.' " And Miss L. fears that "he had given his readers many stones; so many, in fact, that he had only one left—the stone that had formed in his gut."[8] Later he broods over crushed stones and broken rocks. Eventually we recognize these stones (testicles) and rocks (the Rock, Peter's Church): they are tokens of despair.

Miss L. dreams the Christ dream: to heal the sick, to mend the wounded. This "leper licker"[9] is overwhelmed by the desire to fix "all the broken bastards."[10] He is afraid of the risk, however: he is not prepared to pay the cost he thinks "the Christ business"[11] will exact of him. Ultrasensitive to human suffering, he would like to relieve some of it by becoming Christlike, but he also believes that the practice of Christ in the nonbelieving twentieth century has to be paid for by madness and persecution. Thus he is confronted by a dilemma: to opt for sanctity and risk insanity or remain indifferent to the pain of mankind and preserve his sanity more or less intact. The unsavory choice might have been avoided, however, had West gifted him with prophetic powers. Suppose he could have foreseen R. D. Laing's ingenious resolution: in a mad age, such as ours, madness may be the ultimate sanity.

The vast majority of letters that Miss L. receives, "stamped from the dough of suffering with a heart-shaped cookie knife,"[12] are concerned with tribulations visited upon girls or women. Desperate, on the verge of suicide, is a sixteen-year-old, born with a hole in her face where her nose ought to be, who wants to have dates like other girls. Harold S. writes in behalf of his thirteen-year-old deaf and dumb sister Gracie, who is too terrified to tell her mother that she has been raped by a strange man. Sick-of-it-all, a Roman Catholic wife worn out with excessive child-bearing and suffering from excruciating kidney pains, is pregnant again despite the doctor's warning that another pregnancy would endanger her life. Broad Shoulders, in ill health after being struck by an automobile when pregnant, is constantly abused by a psychotic husband. Female humiliation looms up again in the gang-rape anecdotes favored by Miss L.'s associates. One girl is banged by eight casual acquaintances in a lot; another is detained in the back room of a speakeasy for three days, until "on the last day they sold tickets to niggers."[13]

Hypersensitive to these indignities, Miss L. becomes preoccupied with female suffering. Moreover, he frequently identifies himself with pain-ridden women: he fantasies communion with "Desperate, Broken-hearted, Disillusioned-with-tubercular-husband and the rest."[14] In this respect, he looks forward to Fitzgerald's Dick Diver and Greene's Major Scobie. Diver and Scobie seem to share the same dilemma with Miss L.: to be betrayed and trapped by their virtues; to be hoisted on the petard of their sacrificial love. Scobie's love for his wife and for his mistress, both pathetic individuals, leads to adultery, sacrilege, and suicide. Diver's love for his unbalanced wife leads to cuckoldom and crack-up. Miss L.'s love for tortured womankind leads to madness and death. All three of them—the antithesis of Apeneck Sweeney whose indifference to women in pain is colossal—use sexual intercourse, incidentally, as a consolatory device for devastated females. These three, each one at the end of his tether, pose a phony paradox: love is related to self-destruction as cause is to effect. All three novels would appear to celebrate the Wildean epigram: "Each man kills the thing he loves."[15] But that is the case only when one is as neurotic as Miss L., Diver, and Scobie are. Actually, Miss L., no more than the other two, is not destroyed by the Christ vision: he is dragged down by powerful subterranean forces with which he refuses to grapple. He blames his agony on his Christ vision, when in reality he suffers from a variety of psychosexual problems ranging from sadomasochism to homosexuality. Obviously it is more flattering to attribute your downfall to a Christ fixation than to inability to achieve satisfactory sexual identification.

Miss L. has a religious experience at the end of the novel that confirms this misapprehension. He is lying in bed, feverish, on the point of a Raskolnikov-like delirium, contemplat-

ing "the Christ that hung on the wall"[16]—a Christ without a
cross, by the way. (Does Miss L.'s unwillingness to let Christ
retain his cross prefigure his own confusion about bearing his
cross? Does he go crownless because ultimately he is cross-
less?) The room is awash with grace. Suddenly the doorbell
rings and the crippled Peter Doyle, one of his two male
supplicants, emerges on the stairs. Miss L. dashes downstairs
to embrace him, to "perform a miracle,"[17] to gain a sign of
his chosen status, and to demonstrate in this one healing act
his unrivaled sympathy for all those in torment. Terrified by
Miss L.'s distraught appearance, the gun-toting cripple tries
to flee, but his escape is cut off by the sudden arrival of Betty,
Miss L.'s fiancée, at the foot of the stairs. In the ensuing
struggle, Miss L. is accidentally shot, and they tumble down
the stairs in one another's arms, landing at Betty's feet. Observe the difference between the embrace Miss L. intends
and the embrace they achieve. Ironically the latter is the
result of one piercing the body of the other with a bullet,
which recalls the lamppost's shadow in the park that
"pierced him [Miss L.] like a spear."

"It is of course a homosexual tableau—the men locked in
embrace while the woman stands helplessly by," as pointed
out by Stanley Edgar Hyman. "Behind his other miseries
Miss Lonelyhearts has a powerful latent homosexuality. It is
this that is ultimately the joke of his name and the book's
title. It explains his acceptance of teasing dates with Mary
[Shrike's wife] and his coldness with Mary. . . . It explains his
discontent with Betty. Most of all it explains his joy at being
seduced by Fay [Doyle's wife] . . . and how quickly the pleasure turns to disgust."[18]

Additional documentation is easily come by. Finding an
elderly loiterer in a comfort station, Miss L. and a drunken
companion indulge in fag-baiting: they haul him to a speakeasy where they brutally interrogate him about his "homo-
sexualistic tendencies."[19] When he resists, Miss L., overcome
by rage, twists the man's arm until the man screams. Miss L.
analyzes his own feelings as follows: when he first encounters
"the cruiser," he is filled with pity, but when the man's suffer-

ing becomes real to his senses, his pity turns to rage, and he
torments him. Miss L. fancies he is punishing the pervert
because of an ambivalent motivation where suffering is concerned. True enough, but his self-analysis stops short of prob-
ing the source of this ambivalence, his own clandestine
homosexuality. Miss L.'s sexual identity is so shaky that he
feels threatened by the other, and that is why he administers
a frantic beating. The incident recalls the reaction of Jake
Barnes to the sight of homosexuals in a ballroom dancing
"big-hippily." Jake disavows tolerance, even amusement, set-
tling for anger: he wants "to swing" at them—or is it with
them? That he is not sure what he wants to do is suggestively
conveyed by the very way Hemingway phrases the ambiguous impulse: "I wanted to swing *on* [italics added] one."[20]
Closet queens beat up the queens who have left the closet.

Miss L.'s treatment of Betty is further confirmation. The
sight of her sitting in her apartment irritates him. With a
voice "full of hatred," he calls her "Betty the Buddha. You
have the smug smile; all you need is the pot belly."[21] He turns
women into men so that he may ease up on hating them. And
when he pats her shoulder, he does it "threateningly" so that
she instinctively "raised her arm as though to ward off a blow.
She was like a kitten whose soft helplessness makes one ache
to hurt it."[22] Miss L. is genuinely hung up on whether it is
more proper to strike a woman or to caress her.

Straight passion with women is no more Miss L.'s line than
it is William Shrike's. He too alternately cuddles and menaces
them. The two men pick up and are picked up by the same
type, mannish-looking women. Sitting on a park bench, Miss
L. is examining the sky, "like a stupid detective who is
searching for a clew [sic] to his own exhaustion," when he
observes Fay Doyle ambling up the path: "legs like Indian
clubs . . . and a brow like a pigeon. Despite her short plaid
skirt, red sweater, rabbit-skin jacket and knitted tam-o'-
shanter, she looked like a police captain."[23] The exhausted
detective who awaits a grim assignation with "a big" police
captain is not unlike the Shrike, whose name is a form of the
word "shriek," dating a Miss Farkis, who has "long legs, thick

ankles, big hands, a powerful body . . . and a man's haircut."[24] This penchant for male women, of course, is indicative of a sex-role confusion so that Miss L. finds "a strange pleasure"[25] in being seduced by Fay. And Shrike, referring to his wife, goes further, reversing the physiological roles: "Sleeping with her is like sleeping with a knife in one's groin."[26]

Shrike is Miss L.'s foil, perhaps his id extra-mentalized, for it is significant that more than one of Shrike's demonic outbursts is delivered by Miss L. in an earlier version of the novel. And so it is not surprising that they should be involved in an unwholesome *ménage à trois*, with Mrs. Shrike the third party. Miss L. unsuccessfully pursues Mary virtually at her husband's invitation, since Shrike is the kind of man who connives at his own deception. Mary explains his odd impulse to drive his wife into another man's arms: "Do you know why he lets me go out with other men? . . . He knows that I let them neck me and when I get home all hot and bothered, why he climbs into my bed and begs for it."[27] The welcome that Shrike extends to cuckoldry reminds one of similar complaisant cuckolds in contemporary literature—Lawrence's Baxter Dawes, Joyce's Richard Rowan and Leopold Bloom, and Greene's Henry Miles and Victor Rhodes—except that he sets an all-time high for complaisance. The same syndrome, outside marriage, is to be met with in *The Sun Also Rises* where Jake and Mike promote the attentions of Pedro, the virile bullfighter, to Lady Brett, their ostensible sweetheart.

The scene at the end of Miss L.'s date with Mary Shrike brings this neurotic triangular situation to the fore and highlights the Oedipal base. Standing outside her apartment door, Miss L., suddenly aroused by the strong probability that Shrike "heard the elevator and is listening behind the door," strips Mary naked under her fur coat, "kissed her breasts," and tries in vain "to drag her to the floor."[28] After she goes inside, he hides in the corridor. In a moment, he sees Shrike, naked from the waist down, peek out the door. "It is the child's Oedipal vision perfectly dramatized," Hyman comments. "He can clutch at his mother's body but loses her each time to his more potent rival." Hyman prefaces this interpretation with the following: "We could if we so chose write Miss Lonelyheart's case history before the novel begins. Terrified of his stern religious father, identifying with his soft loving mother, the boy renounces his phallicism out of castration anxiety—a classic Oedipus complex. In these terms the Shrikes are Miss Lonelyhearts' Oedipal parents, abstracted as the father's loud voice and the mother's tantalizing breast."[29] The interpretation gains credence from a point Hyman overlooks. What prompts Miss L. to hide, after Mary tiptoes into the apartment, is the sound of manly footsteps within. Miss L.'s withdrawal is described as follows: he "limped behind the projection of the elevator shaft."[30] The verb—inexplicable otherwise, since Miss L. is not lame—hints at Freudian cognizance on West's part.

But there are further Freudian implications here, besides the Oedipal enactment, that Hyman does not address himself to. Ordinarily Miss L. is unable to muster much desire for Mary despite heroic efforts until he intuits the presence of Shrike listening behind the door, and then he is suddenly overcome with passion. On his side of the door, knowing a passion play is going on, Shrike, an auditeur, does nothing to interrupt the performance; he is enjoying it too much. The presence of the other is a mutual condition for the expression of lust. On one level, then, their relationship is that of father and son; on another, they are remote lovers. On the latter level, you have two men acting out evasive homosexuality through a woman. Homosexuality by proxy is not unique with West. Faulkner has Joe Christmas use a woman as the surrogate for his love affair with a man. Common to these triangular relationships is the use two men, to arouse each other, make of the same woman.

Later in the novel, Miss L. plays the same wife-borrowing game with Peter Doyle, another complaisant cuckold. With new partners, however, the rules are observed a bit differently. There is no surface antagonism between Miss L. and Doyle—they achieve communion by sitting silently holding hands—and Doyle is not a complicated person, so he re-

sponds far more openly than Shrike. Doyle even halfheart-
edly jokes about bringing Miss L. back to his apartment at
Fay's command, "Ain't I the pimp, to bring home a guy for
my wife?"[31] And lovemaking is not assisted by the secret
presence of the husband. He is absent on the occasion when
Fay drags Miss L. into her bed where they quickly perform
a joyless, mechanical adultery which floods him with guilt
and qualifies him for the title, least eager cuckold maker in
fiction. Finally Miss L. strikes a Christ note here that was
wanting when he was a third party to the Shrikes. Dinner at
the Doyles' apartment turns out to be Miss L.'s last supper.
He spends the evening preaching the message, "Christ is
love,"[32] futilely trying to bring religious consolation to this
sexually shattered couple. When Peter walks out on him and
Fay starts making Mary Magdalene-like advances, he returns
home crushed. Deathly sick, he undergoes symbolic entomb-
ment: he locks himself in his room and takes to his bed for
three days, subsisting on crackers and water.

The Doyle circumstances are more in line with the thrust
of the novel: sex laced with Christlore. Flowers, colors, so
many things, support this combination. Roses, with their traditionally religious as well as romantic overtones, make the
twain meet. In the final phase of Miss L.'s absorption in the
Christ dream, his room is described as "full of grace. A sweet,
clean grace, not washed clean, but clean as the innersides of
the inner petals of a newly forced rosebud."[33] In this simile,
sex is implicit, merely suggested by the language, which
would be inappropriate in an exclusively religious context.
But for West, or at least for Miss L., the one phenomenon
called to mind the other. In an earlier metaphor, the order
is reversed. Fondling Betty's breast, Miss L. tugs at her nip-
ple and cries: "Let me pluck this rose. . . . I want to wear it
in my buttonhole." When she responds, "Are you sick?" he
launches into a tirade, supplying the missing but expected
link: "What a kind bitch you are. As soon as anyone acts
viciously, you say he's sick. . . . Well, I'm not sick. . . . I've got
a Christ complex."[34] Genet's *Miracle of the Rose* is just
around the bend.

Pink, a less likely bridge, also spans the twain. In their last conversation, over strawberry sodas—"they sucked the pink drops up through straws"[35]—Betty, in madonna attire, confesses to Miss L. that she is pregnant by him. At first she intends to have an abortion, but religion wins a point when they agree to have the child. Moreover, amorous letters are composed on pink stationery cheek by jowl with an allusion to pink toilet tissue. The duo becomes a trio. Eroticism and eschatology are alloyed with scatology: erotic "Latin poetry . . . stained glass windows and crap like that"[36] are to Miss L.'s taste.

William Shrike, especially, derives gratification from this triad. On one occasion, he passes the time of day by talking excitedly about religion, while patting a woman's rump. He trumps the gesture with "a seduction speech," entitled "Shrike's Passion in the Luncheonette, or the Agony in the Soda Fountain." The preamble to the sermon is delivered with a flourish: "I am a great saint. . . . I can walk on my own water."[37] This holy water–unholy water juxtaposition recurs. In a dream, Miss L. recalls "a prayer" Shrike had taught him. "Oh, Lord, we are not of those who wash in wine, water, urine, vinegar, fire, oil, bay rum, milk, brandy, or boric acid. Oh, Lord, we are of those who wash solely in the Blood of the Lamb."[38] And in the course of a visit to Miss L., who is sick in bed, Shrike offers the patient a series of escapes from "the Christ business": the soil, the South Seas, hedonism, and art. The pastoral idyll consists of walking "behind your horse's moist behind . . . plowing your broad swift acres," and sowing seed. "Your step becomes the heavy sexual step of a dance-drunk Indian and you tread the seed down into the female earth."[39] The same formula, excrement fertilizing orgiastic rituals, is repeated throughout. Finally admitting the ultimate inadequacy of all these escapes, Shrike launches his peroration: "We are not men who swallow camels only to strain at stools. God alone is our escape. The church is our only hope, the First Church of Christ Dentist, where He is worshipped as Preventer of Decay. The church whose symbol is the trinity newstyle: Father, Son, and Wirehaired Fox

Terrier."[40] This diabolical comedian is not without progeny in American letters: Updike's Freddy Thorne is his most notable descendant.

The gargoyle characters, the grotesque perception, the episodic action, the strident tone, the theme of the religious quest and prophets in the stammering stage, the ambivalent attitudes toward Christ and Christianity, the impious intimations of religious sacrifice, the nightmarish scenes of sadomasochistic violence, the lurching pace, the corrosive irony, the garish imagery, the serious intent wedded to comic vision, the spiritual carnival atmosphere, and the eerie sense of American civilization coming apart hysterically would make the Christ-haunted work of West unique in American fiction if it were not for the fact that all of the preceding epithets could be applied interchangeably to the work of Christ-centered Flannery O'Connor.

2

Flannery O'Connor came from an old Georgian Catholic family, spent her formative years in parochial schools, and clung tenaciously to an old-fashioned kind of faith. Nathanael West, as we have seen, was born a Jew but forsook Judaism for a flirtation with a kind of Greenwich Village Christianity. The Christianity that O'Connor espoused, culminating in what she called Christian stories "of mythic dimensions,"[41] is quite as special as, if very different from, the offbeat Christianity that attracted West. She seldom wrote about her own kind, Roman Catholics, preferring to deal with rural, Protestant, Bible Belt Southerners, not simply because they predominate in her section of the country, but because "they are people who deal with life on more fundamental, even more violent terms than most people." She adds: "What the Southern Catholic writer is apt to find, when he descends within his imagination, is not Catholic life but the life of this region in which he is both native and alien."[42]

Apart from her predilection for writing about Fundamentalists and Southern Baptists, O'Connor's understanding of and sympathy with Christianity was limited to one of two main Christian traditions which goes all the way back to the Johannine writings in the New Testament. In the epistles, John fixes his attention on the sufferings of the world. In the first epistle 3:17, he poses the question, "But if any one has the world's goods and sees his brother in need, yet closes his heart against him, how does God's love abide in him?" In the Apocalypse, however, John fixes his attention on the eternal glories, compared to which the sufferings of this world were hardly worth a mention. This about-face within the Johannine canon can best be accounted for by the widely held view that the epistles and the Apocalypse were written by two different men, despite the alleged common authorship. Be that as it may, it does not affect the argument: the presence from the beginning of two radically different views of Christianity, the humanitarian and the ascetic. St. John of the Cross, the seventeenth-century Spanish mystic, was perhaps the best latter-day exponent of the second attitude. In *The Dark Night of the Soul,* he concludes: "Hence the soul cannot be possessed of the divine union until it has divested itself of the love of created beings."[43] Fortunately, Christendom no longer sees these diverse orientations as conflicting. The churches recognize that spiritual responsibilities legitimately, if not necessarily, lead to social responsibilities. Today only extremists take the love-God mandate to be irreconcilable with the love-your-neighbor mandate.

Flannery O'Connor was not quite extreme, but she veered in that direction. I am sure that in private life she was not opposed to improving our human condition here on earth, but her writings imply that faith alone, without good works, is all that is necessary for salvation. Since she was not enthusiastic about social action, even in the context of Christian commitment, she could state that it is a mean ambition to write "about the poor in order merely to reveal their material lack."[44] And certainly in the two novels and the two collections of short stories that constitute her fictional output, she suggests that a Christian believer, no matter how sinful, is immeasurably superior to an atheist do-gooder. Her villains are of a kind: she characterizes them as sophisticated skeptics "for whom the supernatural is an embarrassment and for whom religion has become a department of sociology or culture or personality development."[45] Hiding behind excrescences of disbelief, they are wildly defeated by their opposite number, usually a hot gospeler with "a distrust of the abstract, a sense of human dependence upon the grace of God, and a knowledge that evil is not simply a problem to be solved, but a mystery to be endured."[46] Rayber, the schoolteacher in *The Violent Bear It Away,* and Sheppard, a social worker in "The Lame Shall Enter First," are her most thoroughgoing rationalists. The characters whom these ineffectual liberals strive in vain to reform are respectively Francis M. Tarwater, a teen-ager, who, in the midst of delusions about being a religious prophet, is drugged and assaulted by a homosexual in the climactic incident in the novel; and Rufus Johnson, a transvestic reform school parolee, who, even though he is an unshakable believer, defies God.

That O'Connor's fiction is replete with heroes whose personalities are shaped by their attitudes toward the supernatural and sex is, however, most pervasively, if tantalizingly, illustrated by Hazel Motes, the twenty-two-year-old evangelist in *Wise Blood,* her first novel. Hazel, the first of two unbalanced prophets and the first of many religious fanatics who populate the work of O'Connor, is the grandson of "a circuit preacher . . . who had ridden over three counties with Jesus hidden in his head like a stinger."[47] Hazel seeks salvation initially in dreary fornications, then in blasphemy and murder, and finally in an apparent conversion to Christ—a conversion that isolates and magnifies Christ's asceticism while ignoring his good works. In spite of his repeated declarations as to the nonexistence of sin, sin is the most profound reality in Hazel's eyes. His behavior, ill-suited to his words, gives him away. "He felt that he should have a woman, not for the sake of the pleasure in her, but to prove that he didn't believe in sin since he practiced what was called it."[48] When this happens, when a man who does not enjoy sex takes a woman in order to demonstrate a metaphysical position—

namely, disbelief in sin—the action betrays the statement: excessive denial is seen as sly affirmation. This is underscored by the fact that fornicating always fills him with guilt.

The fecal-erotic-spiritual syndrome that we detected in *Miss Lonelyhearts* recurs here. Sitting on a public toilet studying the grafitti on the wall, Haze notices an enthusiastic endorsement:

> Mrs. Leora Watts!
> 60 Buckley Road
> The friendliest bed in town![49]

When he calls on Mrs. Watts in his blue suit and black hat, he looks exactly like a country preacher. Dismayed at what she might be thinking, he falls back again on overly emphatic denial. "I'm no goddam preacher."[50] She responds to this rejection of his vocation by cutting "the top of his ["Jesus-seeing"] hat out in an obscene shape."[51] Even Mrs. Watts perceives that he does protest too much. He likes to believe he fornicates to show his disdain for sin. The opposite is true. Whoring, whether with Mrs. Watts or later with Sabbath Lily Hawks—the depraved fifteen-year-old daughter of a disgraced evangelist—is a joyless rite in his religion. Whoring functions as a divine seek-and-find mission: what he considers the worst sin is indulged for the sake of discovering God so that the Almighty may mete out the punishment that Haze secretly craves above all. This Baudelairean search for salvation has its analogue in Greene's *Brighton Rock* in the person of Pinkie Brown, boy gangster.

The obverse of fornicating for religious consolation is preaching for sexual solace, and Haze finds himself a party to this phenomenon also. When he starts street preaching, his first follower is

> a boy about sixteen years old who had wanted someone to go to a whorehouse with him because he had never been to one before. He knew where the place was but he didn't want to go without a person of experience, and when he heard Haze, he hung around until he stopped preaching and then asked him to go. But it was all a

mistake because after they had gone and got out again
and Haze had asked him to be a member of the Church
Without Christ, or more than that, a disciple, an apostle,
the boy said he was sorry but he couldn't be a member
of that church because he was a Lapsed Catholic. He said
that what they had just done was a mortal sin, and that
should they die unrepentant of it they would suffer eternal punishment and never see God. Haze had not enjoyed the whorehouse anywhere near as much as the boy
had and he had wasted half his evening. He shouted that
there was no such thing as sin or judgment, but the boy
only shook his head and asked him if he would like to go
again the next night.[52]

Paradox, irony, and an authorial foil are all present here.
What the boy regards as mortal sin, he enjoys; what Haze
declares is asinful, he is repelled by. The boy is an unwarped
Hazel Motes: recognizing his fallen nature, he enjoys forbid-
den fruit. Conversely, Hazel, strenuously evading acceptance of his fallen nature, has to deny sin—even though the
stink of it is in his nostrils—and the pleasure attendant upon
it.

The aptly named Haze inveighs against Jesus, "a wild
ragged figure" who forever moves "from tree to tree in the
back of his mind,"[53] with the same monomanical intensity
that he brings to the sense of sin. He dreams of banishing
both from his life. To his sidewalk congregation, he preaches:
"There was no Fall because there was nothing to fall from
and no Redemption because there was no Fall and no Judgment because there wasn't the first two. Nothing matters but
that Jesus was a liar."[54] He adds to this another profanation.
"Blasphemy is the way to the truth."[55] This, of course, illustrates Eliot's famous dictum, cited in connection with
Baudelaire's Satanism, that it is better to do evil than to do
nothing. But in his pre-evangelist days, before he had such
determined traffic with the original sin that he denies, Haze
felt differently: in the army, "he saw the opportunity . . . to
be converted to nothing instead of to evil."[56] The longed-for
conversion to "nothing" never took place, as attested by his

fervor for a new church, his own, "the Church Without Christ: The Church Without Christ don't have a Jesus but it needs one! It needs a new jesus! It needs one that's all man, without blood to waste, and it needs one that don't look like any other man so you'll look at him. Give me such a jesus, you people. Give me such a new jesus and you'll see how far the Church Without Christ can go!"[57] The title is a misnomer. Hazel Motes, who can see the mote in everyone else's eye but is quite blind to any beams in his own, is actually proposing a church with a new Christ. The two most proximate candidates, however improbable, in this grisly travesty turn out to be Enoch Emery's mummy and Haze's automobile.

Enoch Emery, a rasping eighteen-year-old who works as a guard at the city park, is Haze's disciple. Similar to the master, he invariably sees the smutty in a sacrosanct setting. He prays to Jesus to help him escape from the woman who adopted him, and Jesus' ostensible response to the prayer is a provocation to self-exposure. Enoch says, "I went in her room without my pants on and pulled the sheet off her and giver a heart attact."[58] Hyman further explores this sacred-profane nexus when he observes that "in fixed ritual stages" Enoch "must daily have a sacramental milkshake and make suggestive remarks to the waitress, then visit the zoo animals and make obscene comments on their appearance, finally go to the museum and pay his devotions to a mummy. These are Enoch's stations of the cross, as we note from the pun I have italicized: 'We got to *cross* this road and go down this hill. We got to go on foot,' Enoch tells Haze. . . . Enoch also reads the comics 'every evening like an office.' Eventually he finds his religious fulfillment dressed in a stolen gorilla costume, but it is as the apostle of the mummified 'new jesus' that he functions in Haze's pilgrim's progress."[59] Enoch is the self-proclaimed possessor of "wise blood" which urges him to provide the "new jesus" Haze's church needs. His choice is the aforementioned "dried yellow" mummy that the caption alleges was once a full-sized man shrunk from normal height to a present length of three feet. After stealing the doll-like effigy from a glass case in the museum and setting it up in his

room like a god in a tabernacle, he offers it to Haze for
worship. But when Sabbath Lily, Haze's current mistress,
cuddles the sawdust-stuffed skin, making believe it is their
baby, implications emerge that enrage Haze. He snatches
the would-be new jesus from the arms of the venal madonna
and smashes it against the wall. Haze is not content to be a
Joseph figure, even an angry, destructive one.

Another new jesus candidate, one proposed by Haze himself, is a superannuated "rat-colored"[60] Essex, defective in
every way. It leaks water, gas, and oil. Despite these imper-
fections, he extols it as "a good car"[61] and elevates it to
sanctuary status: his vehicle for freedom and mobility, his
soul's retreat, what O'Connor herself calls "his pulpit and
his . . . means of escape."[62] He boasts: "Nobody with a good
car needs to be justified."[63] This car that is more than a car
is not only his temporary substitute for Jesus, but it also functions as a substitute for a woman. The used-car lot owner
encourages him "to get under and look up it,"[64] an invitation
he refuses then but acts on later. (Notice the depersonaliza-
tion of women involved in this conversion of them into a
defective machine.) The most pernicious use Haze makes of
the Essex is as a vehicle of vengeance. He cold-bloodedly
runs over a rival preacher. The murder of his impersonator
is dictated by the need to displace his own strong impulse to
self-murder. Haze's auto epiphanizes his spiritual, sexual,
and suicidal perturbations.

When a policeman pushes the Essex over an embankment,
the author would have you believe there will be no more
substitutes for the Word wounded on the cross: that Haze's
resistance is broken at long last, and he is ready to be redeemed. After his auto is destroyed, he has a terrible but
purgative vision. He feels, even into his bowels, the folly of
seeking salvation in blasphemy, murder, and whoring. He
sees his life for the first time as it is. Contempt for Jesus is the
misleading visible part of his iceberg involvement with
Christ. The murder of his double, the false prophet, is projected self-loathing. Beneath his reluctant dalliance with the
flesh is his deep detestation of the body in general and his

aversion to women in particular. Recall Haze's guilt, at ten years of age, on seeing a naked woman with "a cross-shaped face."[65] His self-given penance was swift: he walked for miles with stones in his shoes.

The view beyond the smashed car affords Haze an experience of terrifying self-awareness. "Haze stood for a few minutes, looking over at the scene. His face seemed to reflect the entire distance across the clearing and on beyond, the entire distance that extended from his eyes to the blank gray sky that went on, depth after depth, into space. His knees bent under him and he sat down on the edge of the embankment with his feet hanging over." When he finally stops concentrating "on space," he resolves to put out his eyes. What he has intuited "beyond"[66] apparently makes ordinary sight so unbearable that he, like Oedipus, inflicts literal blindness and symbolic castration upon himself—except that this is blindness and castration borne for the sake of the Kingdom of Heaven. That *Oedipus Rex* is the archetype for this horrifying gesture of remorse is confirmed by the fact that the novelist was reading the play in the midst of working on *Wise Blood* and acknowledged the influence. Further, Haze has a dream and cherishes a keepsake. He dreams that he flattens his father out in a coffin. "The only things from Eastrod he took into the army with him were a black Bible and a pair of silver-rimmed spectacles that had belonged to his mother . . . the Bible was the only book he read. He didn't read it often but when he did he wore his mother's glasses."[67]

The foregoing explanation of Haze's "conversion" is, for aesthetic reasons, suggested in the novel, never stated. But there can be no doubt that this was O'Connor's purpose in writing *Wise Blood*. Two statements on this score from her essays are incontrovertible. "I launched a character, Hazel Motes, whose presiding passion was to rid himself of a conviction that Jesus had redeemed him."[68] Elsewhere she avers: he does not really disabuse himself of that passion and advocate Jesus "until the car is destroyed by the patrolman. The car is a kind of death-in-life symbol, as his blindness is a life-in-death symbol."[69] Add to this the author's prefatory note to the second edition of *Wise Blood*, in which she describes the book as a "novel about a Christian *malgré lui*," and the intention is unmistakable.

Few critics, if any, doubt the fulfillment of authorial intention. Critics are nearly unanimous in concluding that Haze's self-blinding, and the succeeding chastisements of the flesh —his chest encased in barbed wire; his shoes packed with gravel and ground glass—signify his eventual repentance and attainment of Christlikeness. But is that the case? Does *Wise Blood* actually accomplish what was intended? Does the novel succeed in conveying this meaning? Does Haze's vision culminate in an overwhelming confrontation with grace which converts him, in spite of his lifelong battle against Christ, to the side of the Redeemer? Does he perform saintly austerities to make his peace with God, or is Haze merely a deformed self-centered "saint" who becomes the ultimate new jesus that he prophesied? The evidence, in my judgment, supports the latter position. He burns out his eyes with quicklime more in remorse than to justify any conviction that Christ Jesus has saved him.

Self-apotheosis, by way of unflinching excellence in wooing agony, is the belated discovery but consuming passion of Haze's life. Haze aspires to be a god in pain, rather than to transform his life in Christ's image and become truly a man of God. The transformation that ensues after he destroys his sight—a form of self-crucifixion which is only seemingly a "terrible" conversion to a Savior, stern and all-demanding— is one of ascetic solipsism. Where he is concerned, his landlady, Mrs. Flood, imagines "the outside in, the whole black world in his head and his head bigger than the world, his head big enough to include the sky and planets and whatever was or had been or would be."[70] There is room for only one Jesus and the historical Jesus must abdicate so that Hazel Motes may become the new jesus for his new Church Without Christ. The awful act of blinding himself with quicklime does not in itself demonstrate his belief in redemption. Far from that, it does not even disturb his earlier contention that "the blood of Jesus" is "foul with redemption." He refuses to be saved, and he refuses to save anyone else. His masochistic self-abnegations do no one any good. The only person even aware of these Thanatosic mortifications is Mrs. Flood, and she is merely bewildered by them. There is little evidence that she acquires new understanding or is better for having been an audience of one to his mute agonies. Moreover, the indisputable sign of a follower of Christ is the love he bears his neighbor. But Haze performs none of the corporal and spiritual works of mercy, either before or after his so-called conversion. He never even shows a desire to help others. To the end, he remains an enthusiastic "member and preacher to that church where the blind don't see and the lame don't walk and what's dead stays that way."[71]

In terms of good works, Haze is obviously deficient then as a Christian. He pays no heed to the social aspect of the Gospels. But, in the context of the novel, it is less important than his attitude toward the deposit of faith in the Gospels, since O'Connor gave priority, almost exclusive priority, to this. "For me the meaning of life is centered in our Redemption by Christ and what I see in the world I see in its relation to that."[72] We are back, of course, to Haze's ultimate belief in the divinity of Christ, an intention that I see as not having been realized in *Wise Blood*. As I read the book, religious faith, in the sense of belief in God as the Creator of the world, passes Haze by entirely. What he acquires is a profane faith in himself which alternates between extreme self-hatred and extreme self-love. However, in the interest of fairness to the novelist, some clarification is in order. In view of her short story, "The Displaced Person," it would be an exaggeration to say that in her fiction she places scant store by helping others and that she depicts Christianity as a repository of spiritual obligations which would suffer in the event of any augmentation of social obligations. But the bulk of her fiction comes perilously close to upholding this unfortunate separation. The emphasis can be explained, but scarcely justified, by viewing Haze's loss of sight in another perspective. His traumatic action implies that the only sin is to feel yourself to be at home here on earth and that the heroic alien cannot forget his true homeland. As one who obviously felt herself very much to be a pilgrim and an alien, O'Connor endorses this. Fair enough, but what of the corollary as it applies to Haze: deliberately hiding behind this to disavow involvement and loving?

The quality of violence vitiates the claim the author makes for her protagonist as a Christian *malgré lui.* She defends the use of violence as follows: "In my own stories I have found that violence is strangely capable of returning my characters to reality and preparing them to accept their moment of grace."[73] Violence, it would appear, is necessary to trigger the action of grace in Haze's soul, perhaps because in a corrupt world salvation is possible only through an extreme measure, a sublime act of irrevocable self-sacrifice. Also relevant here is the epigraph to *The Violent Bear It Away,* from Matt. 11:12: "From the days of John the Baptist until now the kingdom of heaven suffereth violence, and the violent bear it away." But what does it mean to say that the kingdom is the object of violence? This obscure Gospel passage still puzzles interpreters, even if it did not baffle O'Connor. She clearly wishes it to be understood that violence is a force used for good by Francis Tarwater and Hazel Motes, enabling them to take the Kingdom of Heaven.

But Christ himself did not display comparable enthusiasm for physical violence. On most occasions, he saw it as a force for evil and repudiated it. His passive resistance to violence, as illustrated by the counsel to turn the other cheek, contrasts starkly with Haze's self-administered violence. In this connection, it is unlikely that Christ would have condoned self-inflicted torture, least of all in the name of perpetuating a barbarity: the self-torture defended by Haze in a dialogue with Mrs. Flood. For when she reminds him that it is neither natural nor normal to wear a barbed-wire vest and that "people have quit doing it," he retorts, "They ain't quit doing it as long as I'm doing it." There is also an implication of self-aggrandizement here: a motive which is the absolute antithesis of Christ's infinite altruism. Haze does violence to himself for trivial, sordid reasons. When his landlady presses him for an explanation, he merely says, "I'm not clean."[74] Under repeated interrogations by her, this is the sole hint, and a thin one at that, that his suffering may have a transcendent aim. But when she asserts that his response is evidence of atonement, he implicitly denies it. And if he ever develops any affection for Jesus, it is certainly expressed peculiarly, since, unlike almost all spiritual questers, he does not identify the search for the good with God. Else he could never reply to his landlady's self-righteous assertion, "I'm as good, Mr. Motes . . . not believing in Jesus as many a one that does," as he does, namely: "You're better. . . . If you believed in Jesus, you wouldn't be so good."[75]

Hazel Motes, from this vantage point, is guilt-riven, not faith-driven, and most assuredly not love-possessed. I hope that I have provided some justification for regarding him, in the last resort, as less a sanctified sinner whose anguish expresses a thirst for transcendental certainty than an irreligious self hater permanently in the grip of a paranoiac obsession with solitude and death.

What interests me here is the gap between what a powerful, percussive novelist, such as Flannery O'Connor, thought she was saying (*intelligere*), with the godlike confidence of a creator, and what—it seems to me—she was actually saying. In exploring the difference between her intention and her accomplishment, I have tried to show that the road taken by her reprehensible sinner is not at all what it appears to her to be, the road to salvation. It is really the route to damnation. For violating the first commandment, making a graven image of himself, Haze deserves the damnation—again as I see it—that awaits him. This interpretation of O'Connor's work as striving against the grain is not intended in any way to deprecate her. I have the utmost respect for her literary artistry. In fact, had she succeeded beyond any doubt with her Good Thief presentation, I am convinced *Wise Blood* would be wanting in tension and driven density, its special qualities. Besides, this saving duplicity, valuable in certain circumstances, is not only in the bloodstream of much of the rest of her fiction, albeit to a lesser degree, but it courses through some of the greatest stories and novels. In American literature alone, *The Turn of the Screw, Sister Carrie,* and *The House of Mirth* are but three samples.

But in "Parker's Back," her last short story—in my judgment her finest achievement and, moreover, one of the best stories in American literature—there is no trace of anti-intentionalism. To please his God-obsessed wife, O. E. (for Obadiah Elihue) Parker has "the haloed head of a flat stern Byzantine Christ with all-demanding eyes"[76] tattooed on his back. But the tattoo only infuriates his wife who, regarding it as "idolatry," pummels him with a broom until "large welts had formed on the face of the tattooed Christ."[77] The intention is gloriously fulfilled. The painful witness for Jesus that Parker bears on his bruised flesh is the perfect, uncanny epiphany for the burden of redemption.

In raising the question of authorial intention, I realize, of course, that I am violating one of the most cherished dogmas in the sect of The New Criticism. The doctrine was promulgated by W. K. Wimsatt and M. C. Beardsley in their well-anthologized piece, "The Intentional Fallacy." They maintain "that the design or intention of the author is neither available nor desirable as a standard for judging the success of a work of literary art."[78] First let me register a point of disagreement. The intention is available when the novelist chooses to make it available as O'Connor frequently does. Thus I used her stated intention for *Wise Blood* as a point of departure. However, the Wimsatt-Beardsley manifesto has merit in their insistence that intention is not desirable as a standard for judging. Any sophisticated reader, I assume, will agree. Design is not to be used by the critic as a criterion; it is an authorial device. Respecting this, the critic has no right, for example, to fault automatically the writer who deviates from his declared design, any more than the critic has the right to praise automatically the writer who executes it well. The intention may have been trivial, in which case the fulfillment will be the same. Conversely, a significant intention may have been ill-focused, in which case an unconscious divergence can be fortunate.

I have scrupulously observed this distinction, I hope, with regard to both *Wise Blood* and "Parker's Back." I praised O'Connor's accomplishment when it was at variance with her intention, as well as when it was one with her intention. It comes down to this: in the novel, she worked better than she dreamed; in the short story, a deeply moving, uproarious work exactly matches a deeply moving, uproarious dream. I have also tried to show that the designing intellect as the cause of the novel is not ipso facto necessarily the best judge of the work designed. Flannery O'Connor concedes as much, when she says, "If a writer is any good, what he makes will have its source in a realm much larger than that which his conscious mind can encompass and will always be a greater surprise to him than it can ever be to his reader."[79]

In *The Violent Bear It Away*, her second novel, the anti-intentionalism is slight, too slight to justify analysis. What does carry over in detail and what does warrant comment, however, is the common evangelical sexual violence. In both novels, murder is invested with implications of black ritual. The circumstances of the vehicular homicide, in *Wise Blood*, caricature the sacraments of confession and extreme unction. The drowning, in the later novel, parodies baptism. When in the act of drowning a feeble-minded boy, Bishop, Francis Marion (named after the "Swamp Fox" general of the American Revolution) Tarwater (a laxative folk medicine), a fourteen-year-old prophet-freak, instinctively pronounces the words of baptism, he performs a grotesque rite in which the sacrament is inseparable from murder. When the act of destroying human life is merged with the act of creating supernatural life, horrific irony ensues.

Ignominious sexual violation and consorting with the devil are joined to profanation of the sacraments as means to an evangelical end. Drab, joyless heterosexuality, always in degrading circumstances suits Haze. Uptight celibacy is Tarwater's lot until the devil in the person of a cruising homosexual, from whom he thumbs a ride, drugs and rapes him. The *unum necessarium* in both cases is humiliation. When they have their fill of it, they burn themselves clean. Although in Haze's case, purification is just a means to self-exaltation. After the rape, Tarwater, in a rage of revulsion, sets fire to the woods where it occurred as a preliminary to burning the woods of his eighty-four-year-old great-uncle, a throwback to the prophets of the Old Testament who came out of the wilderness. At the latter site, young Tarwater, prepared by violent purgation, receives the divine command, "GO WARN THE CHILDREN OF GOD OF THE TERRIBLE SPEED OF MERCY,"[80] which he acts on immediately. In the final sentence of the novel, he sets "his singed eyes, black in their deep sockets . . . toward the dark city, where the children of God lay sleeping." The implication in all of this is unmistakable: the machinations of the satanic agent, culminating in the debauchment of Tarwater, are tolerated by God for the sake of a greater good. O'Connor generalizes: "God can make any indifferent thing, as well as evil itself, an instrument for good."[81] And then the matter is made specific. "In my stories a reader will find that the devil accomplishes a good deal of groundwork that seems to be necessary before grace is effective. Tarwater's final vision could not have been brought off if he hadn't met the man in the lavender and cream-colored car. This is another mystery."[82] No sodomy, no salvation—that is the mystery simply put.

Satanic sodomy as a condition for salvation brings up the nature of supernatural seizure. The question never arises with regard to old Tarwater, who has no physical contact with the supernatural, but it does arise with his great nephew who is familiar with this sort of intervention from almost the beginning of *The Violent,* in the form of an eerie guardian devil who first appears as a rebellious voice in his drunken head, encouraging him to defy his God-given prophetic vocation. For a time, the devil is incomparably more real and interesting than God to the boy who sees the print of cloven hoofs in everything and enjoys nothing so much as a stout tussle with Belial. But the ultimate intimacy, when he is forged for *good* by the phallus of Satan, changes all this drastically.

The critics concur that Tarwater had to be sodomized in order to be saved. Hyman, for example, says: "Even the sodomic rape . . . is right and inevitable: it is at once the ultimate violation of the untouchable anointed of the Lord, a naturalistic explanation for the shaman's spirit possession, and a shocking and effective metaphor for seizure by divine purpose. (Yeats makes a similar use of rape in 'Leda and the Swan.')"[83] In Yeats's sonnet, Zeus, in the guise of a swan, ravishes and impregnates Leda. At the outset of the violation, she is helpless and terrified; before the end, she is "caught up" in Zeus's passion. What the poet implies is that Leda's experience of horror in this violent encounter with the supernatural is compensated for by the godlike knowledge and power that she receives. In *The Violent,* the use of rape is partially similar: Tarwater's involuntary surrender to the rapist is followed by compensatory gain, voluntary surrender to God. However, there is also an important dissimilarity. Leda derives insight and strength from her supernatural seducer. But not so Tarwater, who finds this kind of miscegenation so revolting that he burns the site of his violation. The insight and strength he ultimately acquires comes not from his Luciferian violation but from his visitant's Eternal Foe. The difference is crucial. Zeus is the willing instrument of "grace"; the devil is the unwilling instrument.

The situation that the novelist dramatizes here is sin mysticism—the notion that a protracted apprenticeship of spectacular sin is necessary to the attainment of true virtue—reduced to absurdity: there is no communion with God unless it is preceded by long-term collusion with the Tempter and climaxed by Satanic rape. Religious affirmation depends upon intercourse with the devil, at least metaphorically. Under these circumstances, sexual revulsion becomes a *sine qua non* for salvation.

This phenomenon, the necessity of conferring dignity on sex by associating it with religion, usually the dark side, is also present in many of the short stories. A story of nearly novella length, "The Lame Shall Enter First," deserves special mention, since it is a reworking of the same character triad as in *The Violent:* the humanist, the hell-raiser, and the idiot child. Only the mid one need concern us. Rufus Johnson, a crippled juvenile delinquent who practices transvestism, is redeemed by his habit of tearing pages from the Bible and eating them —even though, recalling Tarwater, he hisses: "Satan . . . has me in his power."[84] But when seduction is practiced by atheists, such as the one-legged Ph.D. and the scurrilous young Bible salesman, in "Good Country People," whose hollow Bible contains condoms and pornographic playing cards, the result is just grubby moral degradation. In the absence of religious affirmation, sex remains a dirty joke: the traveling salesman steals the farm girl's wooden leg.

In a brilliant passage, Hyman shows how the guilty mystery of sex and the redeeming mystery of religion merge inextricably in the mind of a typical O'Connor character. "As the title of 'A Temple of the Holy Ghost' (a Christian metaphor for the body) makes clear, the story is centrally concerned with this equation [of sex and religion]. The twelve-year-old girl protagonist is initiated into sexual mystery by her older cousins, who tell her of the hermaphrodite they saw at the carnival; at the same time she imagines herself a Christian martyr in a Roman arena; when the sun goes down 'like an elevated Host drenched in blood' to end the story, it is the blood of menstruation and childbirth as well as of martyrdom and Christ's Passion."[85] This relationship, sex as the degrading mystery and religion as the uplifting one, remains constant until "Parker's Back." Parker has the face of Christ tattooed on his back to mollify his "saved" and puritanical wife, hopefully to make sex go better between them. But instead of being "struck speechless by the face on his back,"[86] his wife, regarding it as "idolatry," strikes Parker speechless. For the first time, the relationship falters. Religion fails to bail sex out: the *deus ex machina* fails in the role habitually and sometimes unfortunately allotted to it in O'Connor's fiction.

We can conclude that O'Connor follows West in sending Christ to rescue Cupid. Miss L., unsure of his sexual identity and anxiety-ridden as a result, looks to Jesus for a lifeline. Consorting with Cupid is often as humiliating for Haze as it is for Miss L. Both paradoxically seek purification through humiliation for the eventual attainment of self-exaltation. They are less God-pursued than riven by self-fulfillment urges that take the form of playing God. Enlistment in the service of the Lord is a pretext for satisfying compulsions and exercising self-serving power. The God-intoxicated are really self-intoxicated. Somehow the blood of the Old Testament prophets that courses through their veins has become anemic. They are prophets *manqué*.

But the role played by the anti-Christ figures and the treatment of evil are important issues on which O'Connor parts company with West. Shrike is an anti-Christ, because in West's view he washes his hands of social protest and human misery. Rayber (*The Violent*) and Sheppard ("The Lame") are anti-Christs, because in O'Connor's view when they engage in social protest and dabble in human misery they accept the devil's offer of the kingdom of heaven on earth. The difference pivots not simply on whether the two writers consider Christ human or divine but also on which they consider the more important, the ethical formulations of religion or the dogmatic. A related difference likewise attributable to the one's secular humanism and the other's otherworldly orientation is the magnitude of evil. Whereas O'Connor proudly boasts "that my subject in fiction is the action of grace in territory held largely by the devil,"[87] West significantly withholds comment. There is no evidence that he believed in Satan and demonic conspiracies. For him evil was more trivial: man-made, Shrike-produced.

West was a nonsectarian wrestler with Christ and Cupid. O'Connor was a sectarian, American Southern regional wrestler. The final chapter before the conclusion will be given over to a consideration of nine European Roman Catholic writers whose bouts with Love and love were those on which O'Connor tutored herself.

7

The Sexy Cross

The trouble with much of what has passed for Catholic fiction in the twentieth century is that it is simply not Catholic. In the foreground are incense and the confessional; in the background, dominating the action, are sulphur and the couch—or, more precisely, the need for one. In the spotlight is religion; in the shadows, controlling things, is neurosis. Most modern Catholic literature resembles a Good Friday morality play directed by the Marquis de Sade and produced by Krafft-Ebing.

Léon Bloy, Paul Claudel, François Mauriac, Evelyn Waugh, Graham Greene, Charles Péguy, Georges Bernanos, Seán O'Faoláin, and G. K. Chesterton all in one place or another equate religion with sex. The high priest of this neurotic confusion is Bloy: for him women are Paradise. "Every woman . . . is persuaded that her sexual organs are Paradise. . . . She is infinitely right since that part of her body was once the tabernacle of the living God"[1] (*Lettres à sa Fiancée*). But Paradise amounts to pain—"the ecstasy of the Paradise of pain" (*Lettres aux Montchal*) and death—"Paradise is the cemetery" (*Diary*)—so that "Woman is the cross" also. Implicit in these statements is a pseudosyllogism:

The Concept of Paradise involves the cross.
Woman is involved in the concept of Paradise.
Ergo Woman is the cross.

Bloy's liaison with Anne-Marie Roulé, a prostitute who had been a postulant, is the syllogism made flesh. Their relationship was intermittently sensual and holy: "prayers of ten to fifteen hours," he related to Mme Hello, alternating with spells of lovemaking. The suggested identification of copulation with the crucifixion, however, is Bloy's most extraordinary development of the idea: "From ancient times, the male organ has appeared to be a symbol of the Cross. Christ dying on the Cross emitted the spirit. The man having coitus, and in this way crucified in the woman, with a heavy breath emits his seed." (*Le Mendiant ingrat*.)

Paul Claudel also confuses passion with the Passion. The separated lovers, in *The Satin Slipper*, think of themselves as spending what should have been their wedding night nailed to separate crosses. "If I cannot be his Paradise at least I can be his cross," says Prouheze of Rodrigo. "To rend him soul and body, I am quite as good as those two cross-pieces of wood!"[2] And this illustrates the first of three ways in which these writers equate women with the cross. In the matrocentric world of François Mauriac, men suffer on account of women. In *The Little Misery*, a father and son are driven by "the Gorgon," the wife and mother, to drown themselves. "They were close now to the watery confines of that kingdom where never more would they be harassed by wife or mother. They would be delivered from the Gorgon: they would sleep."[3] Raymond Courreges, the narrator of *The Desert of Love*, and his father are related through Maria Cross. They are related by their suffering for the sake of a woman, with a symbolic name, who is lust incarnate for the younger; a God-smitten, dolorous maternal figure for the elder. Mauriac himself was nailed to the cross by his mother. In his autobiography, *Commencements d'une vie*, he confesses with regard to his boyhood that "to live away from what I loved, separated even for a day from my mother," was inconceivable. "Everything which pertained to her took on in my eyes a sacred character and shared in her perfection."[4] And Bloy, in a letter, refers to himself as "a holocaust" offered by his mother to be "entirely consumed by the fire of sacrifice."

In another letter, he writes: "My mother who is a saint educated me for suffering."

In the misogynic world of Evelyn Waugh, women suffer on account of men. Fausta (*Helena*), Aimee (*The Loved One*), and Prudence (*Black Mischief*) are all nailed to the cross by men. Fausta, for converting to Christianity, is roasted alive by barbaric pagans. Aimee is humiliated, driven to take her life by her boyfriend, and her body is disposed of by him in the incinerator of a pets' cemetery. Prudence threatened with cannibalism by her boyfriend—"You're a grand girl, Prudence, and I'd like to eat you"[5]—is ultimately eaten by him. Mauriac is also preoccupied with cannibalism. Blanche Frontenac, a semiautobiographical portrait of Mauriac's mother, is weary with the weariness of "a mother whose children are eating her alive."[6] The spectacle of women at a disadvantage, which so exhilarates Basil Seal, the cannibalistic hero of *Black Mischief*, also provided thrills for the adolescent Graham Greene. "There was a girl lodging close by I wanted to do things to"—so begins a frank confession. "I loitered outside the door hoping to see her. I didn't do anything about it, I wasn't old enough, but I was happy; I could think about pain as something desirable and not as something dreaded. It was as if I had discovered that the way to enjoy life was to appreciate pain."[7] Waugh and Greene share a bizarre erotic interest in cruelty and humiliation.

In the androgynous world of Graham Greene, men are saved by women, and this is the third way in which "woman is the cross." The heroines of the entertainments—thin and bony like small boys—are the instruments of the heroes' temporal salvation. Chorus girl Coral Musker's devotion to Dr. Czinner (*Orient Express*) brings the dying political leader self-knowledge and a sense of peace. Chorus girl Anne Crowder's devotion to Raven (*This Gun for Hire*) brings the rejected boy sympathy, a respite from his long loneliness, and, temporarily at least, an end to the search for lost innocence. The heroines of the novels aspire to be the instruments of the heroes' eternal salvation. Sarah Miles is fired with the desire to be a redemptress. Before a crucifix, she prays: "Teach me to love. I don't mind my pain. It's their pain [that of the men in her life] I can't stand. Let my pain go on and on, but stop theirs. Dear God, if only You could come down from Your Cross for a while and let me get up there instead. If I could suffer like You, I could heal like You."[8] Rose (*Brighton Rock*), in another occasion of God's grace, represents an inverted intrusion of the supernatural: she expresses sincere willingness to forgo salvation in order to be damned with her Luciferian lover. This extravagance of self-sacrifice recalls the offer Charles Péguy's Joan of Arc makes:

"In order to save from the eternal flames
The souls of the damned, I shall undertake their suffering.
I shall abandon my soul to the eternal flames;
My God, give my soul to the eternal flames."[9]

Women punishing men; women punished by men; women saving men: all are connected with suffering. Pain purchases the kind of pleasure that could not be obtained otherwise. Suffering is the coin of the realm for imaginations like these. Greene speaks for himself and his literary confreres when he counterfeits Descartes by having Querry, that burned-out case, observe: "I feel discomfort, therefore I am alive."[10] Péguy has Joan of Arc's spiritual adviser encourage her to hoard suffering for others: "We can and should suffer as much as possible for others here on earth."[11] Bloy, most of all, overdraws his account. "Pain," he asserts in *La Méduse Astruc*, "is everything in life and, because it is everything, we draw from it, as from the inexhaustible bosom of God, all the types of our thought." And, in a letter to Mme Adèle Montchal, he adds sexual interest to suffering: "I asked God continually to send me extraordinary and enormous sufferings, exquisite torments so that I could expiate the sins of all those whom I loved, or would love, or should love, whoever they might be, including murderers and harlots."

The major Catholic writers of this century all believe in suffering connected with sex. We have seen that Bloy and Claudel mix up the sexual act with the crucifixion, that Bloy and Mauriac mix up the mistress with the mother, and that behind Waugh and Greene's view of sex lies a streak of cruelty. To turn the cross into a castrated phallus and to sprinkle holy water on the Oedipus complex is to do a disservice to both religion and mental health. But such imaginations, who are so skewered on the spit of suffering that they see both their own lives and history exclusively in terms of the crucifixion, are fanatical in other respects as well. In *Un Mauvais Rêve*, Georges Bernanos' posthumously published novel, Olivier sums up the creed of Mme Alfieri, whom he regards as the perverse embodiment of Catholicism, as follows: "Love in your language means, 'Help me suffer, suffer for me, let us suffer together!' You hate your pleasure: you hate your body with a sly bitter hate. You've hated it from childhood. Only a child's hate has that character of mean artless ferocity. Your body is the little frog a boy pricks with pins, the captured cockchafer, the stray cat."[12] If one substitutes for the person addressed in this passage the group of writers under consideration, one will have a succinct statement of most of their tortured imaginative patterns.

In the pessimistic world of Georges Bernanos, the demon prevails. "Night belongs to the Devil,"[13] laments the Curé de Torcy in *The Diary of a Country Priest*. Bernanos' entire output supports this contention: satanic black is the symbolic color that dominates the Bernanosian world. The virtue of the "country priest" is defeated by the diabolic wickedness of his parishioners, and the saintly priest of Fenouille is shredded to despair by the devil's apostle, M. Ouine, in the novel bearing his name. When put upon, love and pleasure fare no better than goodness. As M. Guérou, the connoisseur of sin in *L'Imposture*, explains, "the best thing about vice is that it teaches you to hate mankind."[14] And Mauriac, with admiration, quotes Pascal: "What pleasure is greater than being disgusted with pleasure?" Referring to Pascal's relationship to his sister Jacqueline, he says: "In brotherly love, as in any other kind of love, the one wounds, and the other is wounded."[15] Maria Cross, disillusioned, complains that "the people we think we love [are] the passions that end so miserably."[16] Love, particularly the love of God, proves to be discouraging for Greene's characters too. The more Sarah Miles becomes a saint, the more she agonizes and the more she regards herself as "a bitch and a fake."[17] And the more faithful the whiskey priest is to his devotion to God, the more miserable he becomes.

There is a curious inversion of values in the gall-and-wormwood world of these half-Manichaean Catholic authors: for not only do sin, hate, and pain thrive with something like their approval, but they are also more enthusiastic about joylessness, unhappiness, and failure than they are about their antitheses. Humble Father Donissan, another of Bernanos' saints, cries: "I do not wish for glory. I no longer even wish for hope."[18] Péguy, confusing virtue with unhappiness, loved the latter for its own sake. In the *Prière de confidence*, he refers to his "implacable need to be more unhappy."[19] More hesitant, Greene simply recommends that "happiness should always be qualified by a knowledge of misery."[20] Bloy also discerned in himself a natural vocation to unhappiness. "The mere word 'misfortune,' " he writes to his fiancée, "carried me off in transports of enthusiasm." And he adored the church to the extent that he deemed its mission was thwarted and unsuccessful. In the following passage from *Le Désespéré*, religion is battened down with imprisonment, insanity, and poverty: "The Church is shut up in a hospital for madwomen, for having married a beggar on a cross, who was called Jesus Christ." Greene's enthusiasm for failure is more personal. "When success began to touch oneself, however mildly, one could only pray that failure would not be held off for too long."[21] These strange reversals find their "epiphany" in an anecdote about Oxford related by Waugh: "There was a club in Balliol named the *Hysteron-Proteron* whose members put themselves to great discomfort by living a day in reverse, getting up in evening dress, drinking whisky, smoking cigars and playing cards, then at ten o'clock dining backwards starting with savouries and ending with soup."[22]

These life-defeating writers, with their suspect speculations, consistently range themselves on the side of death. In

God and Mammon, Mauriac admits to being made uneasy by a certain type of Catholic criticism that "detected an element of corruption in" his books, but at the same time he does not deny it. "Am I sure that I, too, cannot detect that element prowling over my work, in the way it prowls over cemeteries which are nevertheless dominated by the Cross?"[23] It is interesting that this reference to "the Cross" appears in a life-negating context of "corruption" and "cemeteries" instead of a life-affirming context of redemption and resurrection. In his autobiography, *A Little Learning,* Waugh describes how, as a child, he liked to visit the house of his three maiden aunts because, as he used to say, "people had died there."[24] At prep school, he diverted himself and his friends by forming a "Corpse Club" for those who were weary of life. A few years later, really weary of life, one black night in Wales "at the end of my short tether,"[25] he tells us, he decided to drown himself, only to be turned back by a school of jellyfish. This youthful preoccupation with suicide is likewise evident in Greene's life. Even before he was fourteen, he recalls, in *A Sort of Life,* repeated self-attempts on his life, including "the curious sensation of swimming through cotton wool"[26] after gulping twenty aspirin tablets before diving into the school swimming pool. Finally, at seventeen, he decided to experiment with Russian roulette, only to be turned back by boredom.

Another naysaying symptom is their detestation of the flesh. With Mauriac it takes the form of a throwback to Jansenism. On more than one occasion, he quotes with approval Pascal's concept of marriage as "the lowest of the conditions of Christianity, vile and prejudicial in the eyes of God,"[27] and he speaks, in his life of Racine, of "that certitude fatal to human happiness, that carnal love is evil, evil which we cannot help committing."[28] With Seán O'Faoláin it takes the more oblique form of sacrilegious seductions in holy places. In the short story "The Small Lady," a woman is seduced by a soldier in a Trappist monastery and shot as a spy, with all around the silent cells of flagellants and "the sign and adoration of the Ender of Life."[29] In the novel *Bird Alone,* a pious, innocent girl, who clutches "her rosary-beads for protection"[30] whenever a man comes near her, is eventually seduced in the house of her brother, a priest. Distracted to near madness by the unbearable sense of guilt, she kills herself. In the same novel, another girl, a source of edification to her family and neighbors by reason of her frequent reception of Holy Communion, is unmasked as a prostitute and falls into disgrace. At least two inferences emerge from these examples: first, the spirit is polluted by the body's lovemaking, and even fervid devotion to sacraments and sacramentals do not avail the doomed love-maker. But the second—a conclusion applicable, in varying degrees, to his colleagues as well—suggests that while O'Faoláin sees the body as corrupt, he encourages the sad pursuit of sensuality to the point of investing it with religious significance. This paradox leads us back to the sexy cross—all "gash gold-vermilion" roads lead to the sexy cross—and explains why the "temptation" of Corney, the "Bird Alone," to return to the church during Spy Wednesday services, is described in sexual terms: "I could feel all my solitariness oozing away and a craving in me, powerful as a lust, to yield up everything. . . . The revelation of it drew me erect as a spear."[31]

D. H. Lawrence turned sexual activity into religion; these writers turn religious activity into sex. Both positions represent extremes, but only the latter is profane. Lawrence's characters equate lovemaking with ecstasy and are exhilarated by it; the characters of O'Faoláin, Claudel, Mauriac, and Greene equate lovemaking with joylessness and are depressed by it. Mauriac's Brigitte speaks for the whole clan when she says that one should expect nothing from a sexual relationship but suffering. "All the miseries of our human state come from our inability to remain chaste."[32] Lawrence's Ursula speaks for him when she rejects a sexual relationship grounded in suffering. "I don't want to suffer hourly and daily. . . . I don't. I should be ashamed. I think it is degrading not to be happy."[33] And everyone who cherishes Chaucer— a far greater Catholic writer than any we are now considering—and his earthy Wife of Bath—a woman made happy by sexual love—will agree with Ursula.

Their unhealthy preoccupation with sex is further mani- fest in their anti-intellectualism. Bernanos is the most out- spoken. "Evil comes from the constantly working brain, that monstrous animal, formless and flabby in its sheath like a worm, tireless pumper. Yes, why think?"[34] And Father Cénabre, sunk in degradation, cannot regain his faith until he loses his reason. (Insistence on the fulfillment of this violent condition speaks ill for Bernanos' fictioneering and, more- over, does little for religion.) "All the dark corners [of Céna- bre's mind] were pullulating with a fierce embryonic life— thoughts, desires, and covetings, half-evolved, reduced to their essential, asleep but living in the germ."[35] Since Ber- nanos' Romantic mistrust of the intellect is expressed through phallic and womb imagery, he reveals himself as a trustee of the life-estrangement lodge. Other charter mem- bers include G. K. Chesterton, Bloy, and Péguy. Chesterton exemplifies the same convergence of repressed violence and repressed sexuality toward the overthrow of reason. "Down the steep streets which lead from the Waterworks Tower to the Notting Hill High Road, blood has been running, and is running in great red serpents that curl out into the main thoroughfare and shine in the moon."[36] In a characteris- tically paradoxical gesture, Bloy links an appeal to the dark gods of blood and earth with an appeal to the Dove. "I am awaiting the Cossacks and the Holy Ghost" (*Le Désespéré*). And Péguy's vilification of intellectuals and the works of the intellect recalls Pascal. "And he would reason fallaciously who would hinder the heart from reasoning."[37]

The subterranean trinity of blood, sex, and antireason wor- shiped by these writers determines the view of Catholicism projected in their writings. The ethical aspect, the cultiva- tion of virtue, is downgraded; a spurious supernatural aspect, mystery-mongering, is upgraded. In topsy-turvy "Greene- land," the villains are virtuous and the heroes are sinners. Jolly Ida Arnold (*Brighton Rock*) and the ascetical Lieutenant (*The Power and the Glory*), who lead largely exemplary lives, believe in the achievement of happiness on earth, implement the pursuit of social justice, and promote mental health. Pinkie (*Brighton Rock*), a nihilistic boy gangster, and the Priest (*The Power and the Glory*), a despairing alcoholic, are intended to represent the superiority of the supernatural, at something like its worst, over the natural—represented by Ida and the Lieutenant—at something like its best. Ida and the Lieutenant, who live on the plane of right and wrong and usually choose the former, are no match for Pinkie and the Priest, who live on the plane of good and evil and usually choose the latter. Making a polar antithesis of right and wrong, on the one side, and good and evil, on the other, as Greene does, creates an abyss between the natural and the supernatural that has no foundation in reality. An equally deformed view of Catholicism, sponsored by Bloy, Péguy, Claudel, and Bernanos, establishes a fictional society in which those who suffer are the elect, for they alone, in Bloy's words, experience "the ecstasy of the Paradise of pain" (*Lettres aux Montchal*). Perhaps those who are transfigured by suffering are indeed the elite, but surely those who are demeaned by pain—and their numbers are legion, for many times hardship does not lead to love at all—are not. The implication that catastrophe is the sign of God's favor does little to enhance his image.

Implicit in the literature created by these authors is another Romantic delusion: the past is superior to the present so that maturity is inferior to childhood. Waugh despises modernity. Scott-King, one of his most sympathetically presented characters, teaches the classics on the grounds that "it would be very wicked indeed to do anything to fit a boy for the modern world."[38] The same overweening interest in the past accounts for the heavy Arcadian nostalgia of the fictional Oxford scenes in *Brideshead Revisited* and the real ones in *A Little Learning*. The modern world is to Waugh so decayed from the world of his youth that it seems inconceivable for him to wish any part of that earlier world different.

Like Sebastian Flyte, the teddy-bear-spanking collegian of *Brideshead Revisited,* he is "in love with his own childhood" and "homesick for nursery morality."[39] Bloy too expresses a pained distaste for every aspect of modernity, when he complains "that any social innovation is the greatest possible outrage since it implies the non-infallibility of God" (Letter), and for maturity, when he pictures himself as "one of those beings . . . who look as if they had spent nine hundred years in their mother's womb" (*Le Désespéré*). Mauriac strikes a note of sour disillusionment similar in that it also culminates in a desire to regress to the womb. He speaks of a ten-year-old boy, a self-portrait, clinging to his mother "as if some instinct were urging him to return into the body from which he had been born."[40]

Style is not the issue here. The prose composed by most of this group is so graceful, deft, and felicitous that the style of many of their contemporaries seems barbarously awkward in comparison. Great literary gifts they undeniably have, and they make many incidental points with consummate skill, but they all confuse issues instead of clarifying them. Bloy confuses the emission of semen by the copulating male with the expulsion of the Holy Ghost from Christ's body on the cross. In a less obscene way, Claudel also confuses making love with being put to death. Mauriac and Waugh confuse love with cannibalism. Greene and Péguy confuse self-damnation with self-sacrifice. Bernanos confuses faith with irrationality. O'Faoláin confuses a church with a brothel. Chesterton confuses violence with sex. They all erroneously identify eros and agape. (Incidentally, in *Love in the Western World,* the position of Denis de Rougemont is just the opposite: he so separates the two that he sees them as utterly exclusive extremes—the absolutely evil eros and the absolutely good agape.) In the act of creating literature, they muffle both their intelligence and their Catholicism. These writers warp religion: they dramatize frustrations that result from neuroses and erroneously label the product Catholic literature. While ostensibly glorifying Catholicism, they unintentionally misuse their religion to satisfy ill-understood neurotic needs. They cast the respectable cloak of Catholicism over their aberrations, hoping to disguise them. None of them possesses a healthy, broad-minded approach to either sex or religion.

Conclusion

The ideal common denominator where religion and sex are concerned is love. If we can determine for each of the writers we have treated what they conceive and feel love to be, we can tentatively probe two areas: we can gain some insight into *why* they connect the erotic impulse with the theological and *how* they connect the two. First let us take each writer more or less in turn, and then perhaps we can roughly schematize their views.

D. H. Lawrence recognizes both spiritual and carnal love, but he holds they must be fused in order to be viable. Spiritual desire by itself is unfortunate. We saw him criticize Jesus for making love exclusively a matter of benevolence. To rectify this, he imputes acquisitiveness to his Jesus-protagonist in *The Man Who Died*. To regard benevolence as the primary impulse in love, Lawrence considers an illusion. He describes the most altruistic feelings as inspired ultimately by motives of self-interest. We saw him insist that the ideal of civilized society, "Thou shalt love thy neighbor as thyself," is unwholesome. In this, he agrees with Freud who observes that a neighbor is worthy of love only "if he is so like me . . . that I can love myself in him."[1] But, according to Lawrence, carnal desire by itself, in any form, is equally unfortunate. We saw him dismiss mere friction between bodies as a disguised version of autoeroticism. And he continually attacks romantic passion, at least the branch of it which flowered from the hothouse cult of courtly love, for a failure to consummate. To its polite and melancholy suggestion that desire, not fulfillment, is the best part of love, he counters vehemently that fulfillment is everything. Consummation is of the utmost importance, since it brings both erotic and religious fulfillment. More explicitly than anyone before him, he sentimentalizes the orgasm, in whose "final massive and dark collision of the blood"[2] he sees man's fusion with the divine. The lover is reborn in this mysterious orgastic reconciliation between flesh and spirit.

William Golding stresses the relationship between human and divine love throughout the corpus of his work but especially in *The Spire*. Churches are human structures that have to be divine: The phallus-spire has to be a prayer-spire; the four slender pillars are human lovers with divine aspirations. The vision of the spire which so controls Jocelin shows the interdependence of the two kinds of love to even better advantage. Originally he is certain that the vision is driven by a religious impulse—which it is consciously—but when he discovers that it is fueled unconsciously by a sexual impulse, he agonizes. And he does not resolve the apparent antinomies of love until he abandons the judgmental epithets, innocent and corrupt, pertaining to his vision and perceives that love, if it is genuinely love, is indivisible. The sum of wisdom Jocelin finally attains is that divine love has to be approached by way of human love. Earlier we saw how Golding projects his personal insight into the experience of Jocelin. God has to be found "lying between people."[3] Golding would undoubtedly find Lawrence's statement of the matter congenial: the "problem is not whether God exists, but how shall man find God."[4]

John Updike, much influenced by Karl Barth, quotes as epigraph for *The Centaur*, his third novel, a statement by the neo-orthodox Swiss theologian. "Heaven is the creation inconceivable to man; earth is the creation conceivable to him. He himself is the creature on the boundary line between heaven and earth." Updike illumines this truth—the absolute need for man to commune with both heaven and earth—by commission in *The Centaur* and by omission in *Rabbit, Run,* his second novel, and *Couples.* The plight of the couples, an inability to love self, an other, or God, is a plight shared by Harry "Rabbit" Angstrom but transcended by George "Centaur" Caldwell, who successfully encounters all three. The search for love exclusively through abundant sex is implicitly frowned on in all three novels, because it is unable to make meeting with the God of Calvin and Barth, a God—essentially transcendent, nonhuman, and "wholly Other"—who looms above the human comings and goings. Another strong influence on Updike has been Denis de Rougemont, the author of *Love in the Western World,* who uses the legend of Tristan and Iseult to put down natural erotic passion—acquisitive and destructive in its idealization of women—and to exalt supernatural Christian love—benevolent and constructive in its respect for women. In this view, Iseult is the woman whom it is death to possess. Sharing this view, Updike composes the tragedy of a modern Tristan and Iseult in *Couples.* Piet is married to the unattainable Angela who vanishes the instant she is possessed. Their intolerable situation is an acknowledgment of death's approach, and so they are "ordained for divorce,"[5] says Updike. "What is it that shines from Iseult's face but our own past, with its strange innocence and its strange need to be redeemed? What is nostalgia but love for that part of ourselves which is in Heaven, forever removed from change and corruption? A woman, loved, momentarily eases the pain of time by localizing nostalgia."[6]

Jean Genet's view of love—a jailhouse mystique of carnal love—abounds in absurdities and as such is at variance with almost all traditional views of the subject. Genet identifies God with transgression, instead of virtue, because he muses on the likelihood that God is evil. "At the sacred . . . one neither laughs nor smiles; it is sad. If it is that which touches upon God, is God therefore sad? Is God therefore a painful idea? Is God therefore evil?"[7] The inverted notion that sin is the way to sanctity and evil is proximity to God are, of course, Christian heresies. He is further opposed to Christian thinking when he asserts that the beloved is the mirror image of the lover himself. "You're not my sweetheart, you're my-self,"[8] cries out Divine, the male prostitute, to the soldier Archangel, in *Our Lady*. How unlike Pascal, who terms love of self, sin. And when Divine steeps himself in sexual desire to intensify his egoism, he implicitly repudiates Solovyev who prescribes sexual love as the best antidote for egoism. Still other unorthodoxies are the beloved's required indiffer-ence to the lover; the superiority of homosexual love; hate as the inducement to love; betrayal as proof of love; and the superiority of hate. Archangel has to be indifferent to Divine, if the aim of the latter's love is to be self-sufficient. By the same token, it is easier for another man, rather than a woman, to serve as a man's self-reflection. In *Funeral Rites*, Genet loves Decarnin. But when Decarnin is murdered by Riton, Genet reacts with love toward Riton. In *The Thief's Journal*, when Genet betrays Armand, his beloved, he re-flects: "I . . . loved him too much not to want to deceive and betray and rob him."[9] Finally love is weaker and less effec-tive than hate, and sex is the catalyst to hate. To provoke the audience to hatred, a whore is disguised as the Virgin Mary in *The Balcony*. Genet experiences love as moral inversion in the search for the absolute.

Tennessee Williams has his characters associate love with all manner of things. Within the limits of the characters I discussed, the variety is impressive: for Chance Wayne, love is heterosexual desire; for Sebastian Venable, love is homo-sexual desire; for his mother, love is son-worship; for Christo-pher Flanders, love is death; for Boss Finley, love is power; for the Reverend Shannon, love is God as expressed in na-ture; for Hannah Jelkes, love is the Good Samaritan impulse; and for Alma Winemiller, love is inconstant—first it is self-restraint and later it is incontinence. In the midst of this bewildering variety, however, there is only one instance of authentic love by Williams' standard. If the achievement of interpersonal union is the goal of love then, of those listed, Hannah, who has the aspect of a "medieval saint," is the sole lover. One or two others have comparable sensitivity, sympathy, and understanding, but they lack her moral strength. She has more than pity; she possesses the virtue of compassion: the will to help others, the ability to relieve pain. All the others—especially the male characters who are spurious Christ figures—are desolated and fail to achieve interpersonal union, because their point of departure is either erotic desire or some abstraction. And it is clear that although most of his characters identify one of these two with love, Williams himself does not. Throughout his work, he limits what he calls love to a kind of therapeutic ministry—one that is little dependent upon belief in God, however, when we recall that Hannah is an agnostic—that blesses the unselfish giver as much as the recipient. It is the only real solution for the most pressing problem of human existence: personal isolation. And self-destruction is the price of failure to overcome one's separateness.

Nathanael West, habitually pessimistic, clues us into his concept of love by presenting almost exclusively perversions of love: blasphemy, masochism, and sadism. Judging from the profusion of blasphemers in all four West novels, especially the first two, blasphemy would appear to be the one inalienable right of his characters. In *The Dream Life of Balso Snell*, one character pens a hagiography of Puce, a flea who inhabits the armpit of Jesus Christ; a second is a juggler who balances "the Nails, the Scourge, the Thorns, and a piece of the True Cross"; a third tries "to crucify himself with thumb tacks."[10] These three instances far from exhausting the blasphemous incidents in West's first novel merely typify the multitude. Jay Martin, the novelist's biographer, relates how the characters' stance is West's own: he liked to make Christ the subject of wisecracks. The belated, reluctant Magus disguises himself as a blasphemer. (If West had never existed, it would have been necessary for Flannery O'Connor to have invented him.) In *Miss Lonelyhearts*, blasphemy is the prerogative of Shrike, but this is by no means his sole deficiency in love. He is equally adept at sadism: ruthlessly destroying Lonelyheart's faith in Jesus and shoving him into madness. Miss L. himself oscillates between sadism and masochism. He is usually content to be Shrike's victim, but he victimizes most of the other characters—sometimes deliberately, sometimes unwittingly—particularly those he would most like to help. He fixates on what C. S. Lewis calls "gift-love,"[11] the need to provide for the comfort, happiness, and protection of others. But, since Miss L. fails to distinguish between pity and compassion, he bungles gift-love. His fate, however, is benign by comparison with the fate that overtakes the hero and heroine in *A Cool Million.* The hero is slowly mutilated, bereft of limbs and senses on page after page; the heroine is raped a thousand times. No other literary work provides such a thorough airing for sadomasochism. Nor is necrophilia neglected: the heroine is nearly always unconscious when raped. This is in keeping with West's tendency to identify sexual dreams with death fantasies.

Flannery O'Connor sees love of human beings, whether it be brotherly love or friendship or sex, as somehow interfering with love of God. Where the first two are concerned, her kinship with the sentiment of Thomas à Kempis is plain: "Grant, O Jesus, I may love thee more than parents, relations or friends."[12] Where sexual love is concerned, there are additional qualms and objections. Her writings betray her uncertainty as to whether sexuality is healthy or not. She has clearly not been influenced by an ancient belief of the Stoics that the male seed contains the soul-stuff, but how easy it is to believe that Lawrence, for example, has. Her solitary account of the sexual act, sodomy performed by Satan, manifests her disbelief in the idea that the soul is transmitted by way of seminal emission. Be that as it may, her writings show nothing but scorn for the Freudian insight that sex forces the human personality toward growth and expands man's consciousness rather than ties him down to the untidy passions of his body. They comfort the dragon routed by Freud: the long history of suspicion of all things sexual. Undoubtedly she must have found deeply offensive the words addressed by Heloise to Abelard: "I have ever feared to offend thee rather than God. I seek to please thee more than Him."[13] Creature-love, regularly opposed to Creator-love, is always hazardous.

The last chapter deals with a total of nine writers, Roman Catholics all, who display similar imaginative and theological patterns; hence, understandably similar though not identical notions of love. This makes it possible, even desirable, to lump them together.

Bloy, Claudel, Mauriac, Waugh, Greene, Péguy, Bernanos, O'Faoláin, and Chesterton agree in theory that supernatural love is superior to natural love, which is not surprising in view of their common religious background. Thus you would expect them to measure human love by divine love. Instead, they trim God to fit man. Bloy's cited comment on the crucifixion, with its implication that what is most remarkable about the redemptive act was its unexpected similarity to the sexual act, is the most dramatic instance of this. The Keatsian concept of love as pain serves as a bridge between man-trimmed God and these writers, for among them the expectation of pleasure from sexual love is low. This is attributable to the high incidence of crypto-Manichaeism or in the case of the French writers, crypto-Jansenism. All associate sexual fulfillment with almost as much pain as pleasure. However, this is subject to a qualification: the pain-diluted pleasure is nonetheless somehow paradisic. Sex, dirty transient pleasure, has to be bleached by religion, immaculate transcendent pain. This is the message these writers absorbed almost with their mother's milk; later it was reinforced by their teachers: church authorities, especially Augustine—who went whoring—and Pascal—who never did. In this view, pain and pleasure are inextricably mixed during sexual relations, but so are good and evil. Impure bodily desire must be leavened by pure spiritual desire. The subtle admixture of physiological-psychological and moral issues attaches fault to sexual practice, but since the fault sometimes serves paradoxically as a spur to salvation, it is a *felix culpa*.

While these writers derive relatively little joy from erotic love, oddly they derive even less from mystical love. Love of God, to their way of looking at it, is inseparable ultimately from the imitation of Christ. And since they have basically Good Friday temperaments, the deepest fellowship with

Christ that they can envision is shared suffering. Mauriac's comment, that love of Jesus is most exemplary when the lover is "fastened to the same instrument of torture and exposed to the same derision,"[14] is typical. There would appear to be an imaginative deficiency here which for some reason—masochistic reveling sired by the Manichaean/Jansenistic heritage perhaps—attaches more importance to the crucifixion than to the resurrection. (The generalizations set down in this and the preceding paragraph apply as much to Flannery O'Connor, incidentally, as they do to the writers under discussion.)

Having completed individual compilations, let us summarize positions and then evaluate them. For Lawrence, love is the divination of the spiritual in the flesh. For Golding, love is the divination of the flesh in the spiritual. For Updike, love is a dialogue between heaven and earth. For Genet, love is a dialogue between hell and earth. For West, any kind of love is death-fulfilling. For Williams, benevolent love is life-fulfilling. For the remaining Catholic writers, love is primarily a Christocentric mystery.

Of the sixteen authors, only five are non-Catholics. (Recall that Williams is a recent convert.) The preponderance of Catholics suggests two possibilities: objectively, Catholic writers are more prone to the combination of religion and sex, or I am more familiar with Catholic writers. Assume the former, although the latter is difficult to rule out, since perhaps I am not the best judge of the matter. Acting on the preferred assumption, why is that the case? Essentially it is attributable, as pointed out in the Introduction, to the Roman Catholic Church's traditional insistence on inflexibly regulating the sexual conduct of the faithful. This is not to say that other religious denominations do not formulate moral codes that include sexual prohibitions, but elsewhere ecclesiastical policy is less sweeping and rigid, less binding and enforceable—the mortal-sin backup is missing. But what of the five non-Catholics? Why do they obsessively combine religion and sex? Because of the absence of a common ideology, a monolithic answer is not possible. However, what they have in common, more or less, is a search for the absolute—usually under no particular denominational auspices—conducted along sexual lines. And this does not exclude Genet, who is on an unholy grail quest: an inverted search for an inverted absolute.

Beyond this there is the observable fact that manifestations of religious exaltation resemble manifestations of sexual passion. Mystical ecstasy, accompanied by swooning at the sight of God, resembles erotic euphoria, accompanied by trembling at the sight of the beloved. The very intensity, the tender and fierce aspects, of both experiences frightens people at the same time as it lifts them out of themselves. The coalescence of love, fear, and awe in both provoked primitive peoples to regard the sexual orgasm as a sign of supernatural presence. Since they attached no shame to sex, this gave rise to a guilt-free alliance between the pious and procreative impulses, an alliance that was probably advantageous to both. But what happened in time is succinctly summarized by James Cleugh: "The impulse to worship what can give so much pleasure, as well as pain when frustrated—the 'bittersweet' Eros of the ancient Greek poets—perhaps remained a perfectly innocent combination of desire and anxiety or even terror until its ubiquitous and overwhelming possession of mankind brought it under fire from elderly lawgivers, the 'too severe old men' of whom Catullus complained to Lesbia. For administrators who had lost their capacity for or much of their interest in carnal excitement may well have judged that it took up too much of their group's time, reducing their military and commercial prospects. The notion of guilt in this connection may have arisen in some such way."[15]

The introduction of guilt, for whatever reason, tarnished this symbiotic relationship, with subsequently disastrous results for puritanical moderns. The association of sex with intense religious feeling, as we pointed out, is based on recognition of a common element in both experiences: an extraordinary sense of well-being. The effect is the same but the cause is vastly different, as different as the Beatific Vision on earth and orgasm. Primitives recognized the similar effect but did not distinguish clearly in the area of causes. Perhaps the absence of guilt was based on failure to make the necessary distinction, more likely not. In all probability, even when the distinction dawned, guilt lagged; it lagged until shame was attached to sex. That disparate causes should have a common effect, that the Beatific Vision on earth and orgasm should inspire a common reaction, is no more an occasion for uneasiness than is the realization that the reproductive organ is also the excretive organ. Indeed, where the love that begets children is not considered inferior to the love that begets blessedness, there is no shame. For example, Golding and Updike understand this; writers so unalike, in other ways, as Claudel and Genet do not. Claudel has such horror of the sexual act that he has to bathe it in the perfume of paradise before he may admit it; Genet has such fear of the love that begets children that he never dares undertake it. The sodomic love that begets blessed pain is his "salvation."

In fact, all sixteen authors—and anyone else in our time who associates sex with religion—find themselves essentially in one camp or the other. Those who regard the sexual orgasm as a sign of supernatural *presence* are neoprimitives humiliated by a connection they feel themselves driven to but would much rather flinch from. Those who freely regard the orgasm as a symbol of supernatural *power* do not flinch before sexual pleasure any more than they do before religious consolation. The temptation to place the Catholic writers in the first camp and the non-Catholic ones in the second is an oversimplification, however serviceable it is as a facile generalization. For, no doubt, the recent Greene is more comfortable under the second tent. Whereas Nathanael West and Genet, manifestly uncomfortable in the first tent, actually belong there. As for Lawrence, he is the self-proclaimed leader of the second, even though at night he surreptitiously crosses no-man's-land and fraternizes with the enemy.

I think most of us would agree that the more sophisticated affiliation is the more desirable. Yet, desirable affiliation is quite independent of literary merit, as Flannery O'Connor and, say, Morris West illustrate. (By the way, his foremost novel, *The Devil's Advocate,* has relevance for my general topic and, space permitting, would have made for provocative analysis.) She identifies orgasm with supernatural presence and draws attention to the militant activities of Jesus: the rout of the money changers from the Temple and the threats of hellfire. He considers the flesh created by a beneficent divinity unsullied and sexual-desire innocent, and he draws attention to the meek activities of Jesus: the substitution of love for hate, the exercise of gentleness instead of cruelty, and the cultivation of compassion in place of calculation. O'Connor represents an extreme version of the primitive viewpoint; Morris West represents the ideal of the sophisticated viewpoint. Yet she is unquestionably the greater novelist. They perfectly illustrate the notion—incidental to my thesis—that sound ideology has little to do with artistic creation.

Let us get back to love. For Catholic and non-Catholic writers alike, there is unanimity on the point that human sexual love is sexual desire plus. (No one agrees with Schopenhauer, for instance—although Genet comes closest—that sexual love is wholly biological, no broader than sexual desire.) The terms of consensus are somewhat different, however. The Catholics start with the observation that since both prayer and sexual desire have been called love, the idea of love must include spiritual and physical desires. For the non-Catholics the conclusion is the same, but the initial association is abstract ideals and sex, not prayer and sex. Both concur that the predisposing causes of love are God and libidinal energy, but the issue is primacy. The Catholic authors think of God as Love, so that love among human beings can be fully understood only by reference to God. While not excluding God as a causative factor—for all know there could be no Black Mass without the Mass—the non-Catholic authors, more Freudian-oriented, largely attribute the psychogenesis of love to sexual drives.

In spite of degrees of adherence to Freud, all these writers depart from his contention that spiritual love, in its entirety, can be derived from sexual love; that spiritual love is a mere superstructure reared by repression upon the massive foundation of the sexual impulse. Freud limits eros to sexuality and holds that it is the only principle of love operative in man, a position anticipated to some extent by Schopenhauer. All find Jung more congenial. Jung denies that all love is either sexual desire or a sublimation of same. In *Two Essays on Analytical Psychology,* he opts for a spiritual eros, dividing natural love into carnal eros and spiritual eros. "Eros is a questionable fellow and will always remain so. . . . He belongs on one side to man's primordial animal nature which will endure as long as man has an animal body. On the other side he is related to the highest forms of the spirit. But he only thrives when spirit and instinct are in right harmony."[16] Fiction deals primarily with concretions, not concepts, and so there is risk inherent in asserting that all the writers under scrutiny instinctively march to the tune of Jung. But that would certainly appear to be the case.

The next step, dividing supernatural love into agape and eros, is where they falter. They mostly combine carnal, not spiritual, eros with agape. By doing this, they cause unnecessary confusion between religion and sex: they trip over the only harmonious relationship that can exist between eros and agape. The alternative combining spiritual eros with agape is the solution. When agape is bracketed with the higher form of eros, God the Father, pure spirit, is properly glorified. Otherwise his divinity is obfuscated by carnal encrustations. This solution is faithful to the earliest revealed account of man: man made in God's image and likeness, not the other way around. The substitution of the kind of eros indigenous to supernatural love can be construed as a double blessing: at once a form of perfecting eros and avoiding undue anthropomorphism. The condition then for the correct bifurcation of supernatural love is the acceptance of bifurcated eros on the level of natural love.

That this acceptance can lead to an exemplary reconciliation between eros and agape is beautifully illustrated by the Pauline text on nuptial symbolism. Notice how Paul makes the conjugal union of man and wife a symbol for the spiritual union between Christ and the church: "Husbands love your wives, as Christ also loved the church. . . . So also ought men to love their wives as their own bodies. He that loveth his wife loveth himself. For no man ever hated his own flesh; but nourisheth it and cherisheth it, as also Christ doth the church: Because we are members of his body, of his flesh, and of his bones. . . . This is a great sacrament; but I speak in Christ and in the church." (Eph. 5:25–32.) On the natural plane, Paul commends both carnal eros—a man loving his wife—and spiritual eros—self-love. On the supernatural plane, he commends agape—Mystical Body love—with spiritual eros as the link. Spiritual eros is inchoate agape.

However, to oppose the inclusion of any vestige of the eros motif in the Christian notion of love is to find eros and agape irreconcilable. Denis de Rougemont's extreme Protestant view, owing something to Nygren and perhaps ultimately to Luther, illustrates this. In both *Love in the Western World* and *Love Declared,* de Rougemont assigns eros, understood as a univocal reality, and agape to warring roles. As exemplified in the myths of Tristan and Don Juan, pagan eros is adulterous passion, subversive to marriage, in love with love itself, and so selfish, evil, suicidal. Christian agape is orthodox love between man and God as well as human beings, in which the lover is in love with the beloved, and so altruistic, good, life-sustaining. How dissatisfying is his absolute contrast between eros and agape; how unlike Paul's triptych view, implying a double eros at peace with agape. Paul refused to cast the western world into the dichotomy of passionate vs. orthodox love. This is not to claim for Paul a completely modern view of love. Of course, he examined love against the background of religious presuppositions. But in another way—by describing love between male and female as neither diseased nor supernatural—he anticipated the twentieth century: making it possible to analyze love in relation to concepts of health and sanity. De Rougemont inhabits a past that never was. Paul was a maker of the future.

Historically, love has always been viewed in a tendential way, as a desire, and usually in an evaluative way, as a good, as well. With regard to the latter, there is a necessary distinction. Prior to modernity, whenever judgments were pronounced, they were based on moral or religious presuppositions; since the age of psychology the new standard is mental health. Let us glance at both spheres of judgment so as to apply them generally to the writers under discussion.

Where the relationship between sexual desire and love is concerned, there are two unhealthy views and one healthy one. To equate love and sexual desire is to err; to find them mutually exclusive is also to err. To conclude that sexual desire is never more than part of love—they should be related as species to genus—is to take the only sane view. In theory at least, none of the writers we have discussed urges either of the first two positions. But in the practice of their fiction, we have noted the intrusion of multiple aberrations.

Analyzing love in the light of medical assumptions is, of course, not necessarily superior to examining love in the light of ethical assumptions. The old standard is as efficacious as the new, if it is judiciously used. Here too there are valid and invalid approaches. Take the relationship between sexual love and religious love. To regard celibacy as per se more meritorious than marriage is to nod; to equate celibacy with unacknowledged anxieties about pederasty is also to nod. Enlightenment in this sphere comes from admitting two propositions. Eros and agape are the ingredients in both religious and sexual love, with agape to the fore in religious love and vice versa. The two aforementioned types of eros are involved in sexual love. Carnal eros incites a man to desire a woman as a sexual object. But if sexual desire is to expand into sexual love, spiritual eros must incite the man to desire the woman as a person. And at this point, agape becomes a minor motif in sexual love, since desiring a woman as a person is implicit recognition that she was created by God, who is Love, in his own image and likeness. The fictioneering practices that we have observed frequently skip the transitionary step with unfortunate results. The second proposition, related to the first, allows that religious love can be derived from sexual love and vice versa. The fictioneering practices that we have observed present their fair share of sluts who become saints, for example, and holy fools who discover their bodies.

In human eyes, the event of the incarnation contributed to the confusion between divine love and carnal love. At the hushed moment in time when the Word became flesh, the terms "divine" and "carnal" ceased to be incommensurable. And this had an extraordinary impact on the history of Western spirituality. The language that mystics fashioned in order to describe their experience of union with God increasingly reverted to the bold imagery of eroticism. Now there is nothing unseemly about employing unabashedly the language of human passion in the presence of the Passion, provided the user is aware that he is resorting to a principle of analogy. The usage is not justified, however, when there is more than a linguistic similarity to genital yearning. Mystics who unwittingly owe their gravely magnificent visions to sexual repression merely compound the confusion between religion and sex. Any authentic connection between the two must begin with recognition of their different objects of desire.

For a nightcap, I should like to quote the most succinct and felicitous distinction I know of in this area. The words are those of the late W. H. Auden. They appeared posthumously. "I think I understand why, when theologians like Gregorius, St. Bernard, and St. Peter Damian wanted to describe this experience [mystical union], granted to very few people . . . they should have resorted to the erotic poetry of the Song of Songs. What they seem to be saying is that there are only two human experiences in which ego-consciousness is completely obliterated, the mystical union and the sexual orgasm. The difficulty about this is that the average reader is apt to take what they intended to be an analogy as an identity and to imagine the mystical union as being itself an erotic experience. Thus, when one looks at Bernini's famous sculpture of St. Teresa in ecstasy, what one sees is a woman in orgasm. I'm perfectly certain that the two experiences must be totally different. Agape and Eros are not the same."[17]

Notes

Introduction

1. "Talk with Federico Fellini," *The New York Times Arts and Leisure*, Sec. 2, Sept. 7, 1969, p. 1.
2. Malcolm Muggeridge, *Jesus Rediscovered* (Doubleday & Company, Inc., 1969), p. 48.
3. *Ibid.*, p. 205.
4. Robert Coover, "Notes from the Underground," *Evergreen Review*, Vol. XV, No. 89 (May 1971), p. 74.
5. Andrew Greeley, "The Sacred and the Psychedelic," *The Critic*, Vol. XXVII, No. 5 (April–May 1969), pp. 24–32.
6. John Allegro, *The Sacred Mushroom and the Cross* (London: Hodder and Stoughton, Ltd., 1970), p. xi.
7. J. S. Cooper, "Letters," *The New York Review of Books*, April 22, 1971, p. 61.
8. William Graham Cole, *Sex and Love in the Bible* (Association Press, 1959), p. 181.
9. Herodotus, *Herodotus*, tr. by A. D. Godley (The Loeb Classic Library, 1920), Book I, pp. 251–253.
10. Plato, *The Works of Plato*, ed. by Irwin Edman (Modern Library, Inc., 1928), p. 357.
11. Nicholas Perella, *The Kiss Sacred and Profane* (University of California Press, 1969), p. 282.
12. Cole, *op. cit.*, pp. 292–293.
13. Perella, *op. cit.*, p. 296.
14. William E. Phipps, *Was Jesus Married?* (Harper & Row, Publishers, Inc., 1970), p. 196.
15. Eugene Kennedy, "Sexuality: Who Has the Problem?" *The*

Critic, Vol. XXVII, No. 6 (June–July 1969), p. 26.

16. All quotations in this paragraph are drawn from James Cleugh, *Love Locked Out* (London: Hamlyn House, 1970), pp. 9, 156, 264–265.
17. *Ibid.,* p. 27.
18. *Ibid.,* p. 90.
19. *Ibid.,* p. 96.
20. *Ibid.,* p. 110.
21. *Ibid.,* p. 127.
22. *Ibid.,* p. 129.
23. Andreas Capellanus, *De amore,* ed. by S. Battaglia (Rome: 1947), p. 212.
24. Perella, *op. cit.,* p. 266.
25. Jaufré Rudel, *Les Chansons de Jaufré Rudel,* ed. by A. Jeanroy (Paris: 1924), p. 5.
26. Augustine, *Basic Writings of St. Augustine,* ed. by Whitney J. Oates (Random House, Inc., 1948), Vol. I, p. 89.
27. *Carmina Burana: Lateinische und deutsche Lieder und Gedichte einer Handschrift des XIII Jahrhunderts aus Benedictbeuern* (Stuttgart: 1847), p. 132.
28. James Wilhelm, *The Cruelest Month: Spring, Nature, and Love in Classical and Medieval Lyrics* (Yale University Press, 1965), p. 132.
29. Perella, *op. cit.,* p. 139.
30. R. A. Nicholson, *Studies in Islamic Mysticism* (Cambridge, England: Cambridge University Press, 1921), pp. 163–164.
31. Perella, *op. cit.,* p. 115.
32. *Ibid.,* p. 247.

1

Lawrence's *The Man Who Died:* The Heavenly Cock

1. D. H. Lawrence, *The Collected Letters of D. H. Lawrence,* ed. by Harry T. Moore (The Viking Press, Inc., 1962), p. 420.
2. *Ibid.,* p. 23.
3. *Ibid.,* p. 173.
4. *Ibid.,* p. 975.
5. *Ibid.,* p. 1115.
6. D. H. Lawrence, *The Rainbow* (Modern Library, Inc., n.d.), p. 264.
7. Lawrence, *The Collected Letters,* p. 76.
8. William Troy, *Selected Essays* (Rutgers University Press, 1967), p. 121.
9. D. H. Lawrence, *The Man Who Died,* in *The Short Novels*

(London: William Heinemann, Ltd., 1956), Vol. II, p. 7.
10. *Ibid.*, p. 8.
11. *Ibid.*, p. 10.
12. *Ibid.*, pp. 13–14.
13. Lawrence, *The Collected Letters*, p. 139.
14. *Ibid.*, p. 467.
15. *Ibid.*, p. 431.
16. *Ibid.*, p. 327.
17. *Ibid.*, p. 317.
18. *Ibid.*, p. 251.
19. *Ibid.*, p. 291.
20. *Ibid.*, p. 280.
21. *Ibid.*, p. 129.
22. *Ibid.*, p. 829.
23. Lawrence, *The Rainbow*, p. 223.
24. Lawrence, *The Man Who Died*, p. 30.
25. Lawrence, *The Collected Letters*, p. 811.
26. *Ibid.*, p. 763.
27. *Ibid.*, pp. 531–532.
28. *Ibid.*, p. 981.
29. Lawrence, *The Man Who Died*, p. 41.
30. *Ibid.*, pp. 43–44.
31. Lawrence, *The Collected Letters*, p. 180.
32. *Ibid.*, p. 967.
33. *Ibid.*, p. 1062.
34. *Ibid.*, p. 1047.
35. *Ibid.*, p. 303.
36. *Ibid.*, p. 726.
37. *Ibid.*, p. 972.
38. *Ibid.*, p. 1111.
39. *Ibid.*, p. 319.
40. *Ibid.*, p. 725.
41. *Ibid.*, p. 466.
42. *Ibid.*, p. 476.
43. *Ibid.*, p. 861.
44. *Ibid.*, p. 1164.
45. Lawrence, *The Rainbow*, p. 322.
46. Lawrence, *The Collected Letters*, p. 301.
47. *Ibid.*, pp. 459–460.
48. *Ibid.*, p. 459.
49. *Ibid.*, p. 285.
50. *Ibid.*, p. 492.
51. Bernard Shaw, *Man and Superman* (Penguin Books, Inc., 1952), p. 259.
52. Lawrence, *The Collected Letters*, p. 112.

53. *Ibid.*, p. 123.
54. *Ibid.*, p. 565.
55. Lawrence, *The Man Who Died*, p. 27.
56. *Ibid.*, p. 30.
57. *Ibid.*, p. 34.
58. Lawrence, *The Collected Letters*, p. 119.
59. Lawrence, *The Man Who Died*, p. 28.
60. *Ibid.*, p. 16.
61. *Ibid.*, p. 47.
62. *Ibid.*, p. 17.
63. *Ibid.*, p. 21.
64. Lawrence, *The Rainbow*, p. 172.
65. *Ibid.*, p. 159.
66. William Gass, "Review of Phoenix and Phoenix II," *The New York Review of Books*, Aug. 1, 1968, p. 4.
67. Lawrence, *The Collected Letters*, p. 620.

2
Golding's *The Spire:* The Prayer and the Phallus

1. William Golding, *The Spire* (Harcourt, Brace and World, Inc., 1964), p. 115.
2. *Ibid.*, p. 4.
3. *Ibid.*, p. 7.
4. *Ibid.*, p. 86.
5. *Ibid.*, p. 107.
6. *Ibid.*, p. 123.
7. *Ibid.*, p. 122.
8. *Ibid.*, p. 95.
9. *Ibid.*, p. 213.
10. *Ibid.*, p. 215.
11. *Ibid.*, p. 181.
12. *Ibid.*, p. 214.
13. *Ibid.*, p. 212.
14. *Ibid.*, p. 17.
15. *Ibid.*, p. 31.
16. *Ibid.*, p. 83.
17. *Ibid.*, p. 103.
18. *Ibid.*, p. 162.
19. *Ibid.*, p. 186.
20. *Ibid.*, p. 214.
21. *Ibid.*, p. 215.
22. *Ibid.*, pp. 196–197.
23. *Ibid.*, p. 215.

24. *Ibid.*
25. *Ibid.*, p. 207.
26. *Ibid.*, p. 116.
27. *Ibid.*, p. 64.
28. *Ibid.*, p. 112.
29. *Ibid.*, p. 214.
30. *Ibid.*, p. 212.
31. Bernard Shaw, *Major Critical Essays: The Quintessence of Ibsenism* (London: Constable, 1932), p. 123.
32. Henrik Ibsen, *The Master Builder*, in *Plays by Henrik Ibsen* (Modern Library, Inc., 1950), p. 377.
33. Golding, *op cit.*, p. 154.
34. *Ibid.*, p. 151.
35. Ibsen, *op cit.*, p. 378.

3
John Updike: Between Heaven and Earth

1. Lewis Nichols, "Talk with John Updike," *The New York Times Book Review*, Sec. 7, April 7, 1968, p. 34.
2. John Updike, *The Poorhouse Fair* (Alfred A. Knopf, Inc., 1958), p. 96.
3. *Ibid.*, p. 112.
4. *Ibid.*, p. 113.
5. *Ibid.*, p. 16.
6. Johannes Munck, *The Anchor Bible: The Acts of the Apostles*, rev. by William Albright and C. S. Mann (Doubleday & Company, Inc., 1967), p. 63.
7. Updike, *The Poorhouse Fair*, p. 65.
8. Raymond F. Stoll, *The Gospel According to Luke: A Study of the Third Gospel with a Translation and Commentary* (Frederick Pustet Company, Inc., 1931), pp. 381–382.
9. Updike, *The Poorhouse Fair*, p. 134.
10. *Ibid.*, p. 14.
11. *Ibid.*, p. 158.
12. *Ibid.*, p. 95.
13. *Ibid.*, p. 14.
14. *Ibid.*, p. 16.
15. *Ibid.*, p. 184.
16. *Ibid.*, p. 14.
17. *Ibid.*, pp. 9–10.
18. *Ibid.*, p. 11.
19. *Ibid.*, p. 33.
20. *Ibid.*, p. 34.

21. *Ibid.,* p. 35.
22. Nichols, *loc. cit.,* p. 34.
23. John Updike, *Couples* (Alfred A. Knopf, Inc., 1968), p. 407.
24. *Ibid.,* p. 215.
25. *Ibid.,* p. 370.
26. *Ibid.,* p. 54.
27. Nichols, *loc. cit.,* p. 34.
28. Bruce Vawter, *The Path Through Genesis* (Sheed & Ward, Inc., 1956), p. 152.
29. Updike, *Couples,* p. 444.
30. *Ibid.,* p. 327.
31. *Ibid.,* p. 348.
32. *Ibid.,* p. 330.
33. *Ibid.,* p. 347.
34. *Ibid.,* p. 139.
35. *Ibid.,* p. 302.
36. *Ibid.,* p. 200.
37. *Ibid.,* p. 224.
38. *Ibid.,* p. 441.
39. Nichols, *loc. cit.,* p. 35.
40. Updike, *Couples,* p. 17.
41. *Ibid.,* p. 452.
42. *Ibid.,* p. 419.
43. *Ibid.,* p. 310.
44. *Ibid.,* p. 277.
45. Nichols, *loc. cit.,* p. 34.
46. Updike, *Couples,* p. 31.
47. *Ibid.,* p. 372.
48. *Ibid.,* p. 240.
49. *Ibid.,* p. 146.
50. *Ibid.,* p. 7.
51. *Ibid.,* p. 299.
52. *Ibid.,* p. 242.
53. *Ibid.,* p. 169.
54. *Ibid.,* p. 407.
55. *Ibid.,* p. 371.
56. *Ibid.,* p. 242.
57. *Ibid.,* p. 370.
58. *Ibid.,* p. 371.
59. *Ibid.,* p. 402.
60. *Ibid.,* p. 412.
61. *Ibid.,* p. 407.
62. *Ibid.,* p. 408.
63. *Ibid.,* p. 415.
64. *Ibid.,* p. 421.

65. *Ibid.,* p. 207.
66. *Ibid.,* p. 322.
67. *Ibid.,* p. 313.
68. *Ibid.,* p. 384.
69. *Ibid.,* p. 199.
70. *Ibid.,* p. 254.
71. *Ibid.,* p. 273.
72. *Ibid.,* p. 338.
73. *Ibid.,* pp. 393, 399.
74. *Ibid.,* p. 402.
75. *Ibid.,* pp. 81–82.
76. *Ibid.,* p. 329.
77. *Ibid.,* p. 330.
78. *Ibid.,* p. 347.
79. *Ibid.,* p. 336.
80. *Ibid.,* p. 346.
81. *Ibid.,* p. 451.
82. *Ibid.,* p. 265.
83. Nichols, *loc. cit.,* p. 34.
84. Updike, *Couples,* p. 319.
85. *Ibid.,* pp. 30–32.
86. *Ibid.,* p. 22.
87. *Ibid.,* p. 220.
88. *Ibid.,* p. 323.
89. *Ibid.,* p. 343.
90. *Ibid.,* p. 435.
91. *Ibid.,* p. 389.

4
Tennessee Williams: God, Sex, and Death

1. Tennessee Williams, "Kingdom of Earth," *Esquire*, Vol. LXVII, No. 2 (Feb. 1967), p. 100.
2. Tennessee Williams, *Suddenly Last Summer* (New Directions, 1958), p. 21.
3. Tennessee Williams, *Summer and Smoke* (New Directions, 1948), p. 128.
4. Tennessee Williams, *Camino Real* (New Directions, 1953), p. 17.
5. *Ibid.,* p. 113.
6. *Ibid.,* p. 123.
7. *Ibid.,* p. 133.
8. Williams, *Suddenly Last Summer,* p. 21.
9. *Ibid.,* p. 40.

10. *Ibid.*, p. 17.
11. Tennessee Williams, *Sweet Bird of Youth* (New Directions, 1959), p. 98.
12. *Ibid.*, p. 96.
13. *Ibid.*, p. 95.
14. Tennessee Williams, *The Night of the Iguana* (New Directions, 1962), p. 57.
15. *Ibid.*, p. 55.
16. *Ibid.*, p. 107.
17. Tennessee Williams, *The Milk Train Doesn't Stop Here Anymore* (New Directions, 1964), p. 111.
18. Tennessee Williams, *The Gnädiges Fräulein*, in *Dragon Country: A Book of Plays* (New Directions, 1970), p. 261.
19. Friedrich Nietzsche, *The Complete Works of Friedrich Nietzsche*, ed. by Oscar Levy (Russell & Russell Publishers, 1964), Vol. XI, p. 325.
20. Williams, *Suddenly Last Summer*, p. 17.
21. Williams, *The Night of the Iguana*, p. 122.
22. Williams, *The Milk Train*, p. 110.
23. Williams, *The Night of the Iguana*, p. 99.
24. *Ibid.*, p. 98.
25. Williams, *The Milk Train*, p. 112.
26. Tennessee Williams, *Orpheus Descending* (New Directions, 1958), p. 166.
27. Williams, *The Night of the Iguana*, p. 110.
28. "Noted Playwright Becomes Catholic," *The Catholic News*, Jan. 16, 1969, p. 4.

5
Jean Genet: Counterfeit Saint

1. Jean Genet, *The Thief's Journal*, tr. by Bernard Frechtman (Grove Press, Inc., 1964), p. 92.
2. *Ibid.*, p. 84.
3. *Ibid.*, p. 163.
4. Jean Genet, *The Miracle of the Rose*, tr. by Bernard Frechtman (Grove Press, Inc., 1965), p. 118.
5. *Ibid.*, pp. 247, 248.
6. *Ibid.*, p. 121.
7. *Ibid.*, p. 248.
8. *Ibid.*, p. 192.
9. *Ibid.*, p. 59.
10. *Ibid.*, p. 334.
11. *Ibid.*, p. 337.

12. *Ibid.*, p. 344.
13. *Ibid.*, p. 2.
14. *Ibid.*, p. 198.
15. Jean Genet, *Our Lady of the Flowers,* tr. by Bernard Frechtman (Grove Press, Inc., 1963), p. 280.
16. *Ibid.*, p. 285.
17. *Ibid.*, p. 288.
18. *Ibid.*, p. 302.
19. Genet, *The Journal,* p. 194.
20. Genet, *Our Lady,* p. 253.
21. Genet, *Miracle,* p. 237.
22. Quoted by Jean-Paul Sartre in his book, *Saint Genet,* tr. by Bernard Frechtman (George Braziller, Inc., 1963), p. 398.
23. Genet, *The Journal,* p. 244.
24. *Ibid.*, pp. 206, 207.
25. Sarte, *Saint Genet,* p. 191.
26. Genet, *Our Lady,* p. 85.
27. Genet, *The Journal,* p. 86.
28. *Ibid.*, p. 22.
29. Jean Genet, *Funeral Rites,* tr. by Bernard Frechtman (Grove Press, Inc., 1969), p. 248.
30. Genet, *The Journal,* p. 173.
31. Genet, *Miracle,* p. 268.
32. *Ibid.*, p. 33.
33. Genet, *The Journal,* p. 70.
34. *Ibid.*, p. 82.
35. Genet, *Our Lady,* pp. 201–202.
36. *Ibid.*, p. 267.
37. *Ibid.*, p. 311.
38. *Ibid.*, p. 198.
39. Genet, *The Journal,* p. 268.
40. Genet, *Funeral Rites,* p. 224.
41. Genet, *The Journal* (Foreword), p. 8.
42. *Ibid.*, p. 9.
43. Genet, *Miracle,* p. 202.
44. Genet, *Our Lady,* p. 91.
45. *Ibid.*, p. 266.
46. Sartre, *Saint Genet,* p. 398.
47. Genet, *Miracle,* p. 244.
48. Genet, *Our Lady,* pp. 267, 268.
49. *Ibid.*, p. 267.
50. Genet, *The Journal,* p. 181.
51. *Ibid.*, p. 43.
52. *Ibid.*, p. 128.
53. Genet, *Our Lady,* p. 166.

54. *Ibid.*, p. 69.
55. Genet, *Funeral Rites*, p. 81.
56. Genet, *The Journal*, p. 43.
57. Genet, *Our Lady*, p. 116.
58. Genet, *The Journal*, p. 246.
59. Genet, *Miracle*, p. 69.
60. *Ibid.*, p. 332.
61. Genet, *Our Lady*, p. 71.
62. *Ibid.*, p. 307.
63. *Ibid.*, p. 144.
64. *Ibid.*, p. 112.
65. *Ibid.*, p. 155.
66. *Ibid.*, p. 94.
67. *Ibid.*, p. 197.
68. *Ibid.*, p. 162.
69. Genet, *Funeral Rites*, p. 59.
70. Genet, *The Journal*, p. 153.
71. *Ibid.*, pp. 60–61.
72. *Ibid.*, p. 169.
73. "Two Loves," *Aesthetes and Decadents of the 1890's,* ed. by Karl Beckson (Vintage Books, Inc., 1966), p. 82.
74. Genet, *Our Lady*, p. 139.
75. Genet, *Funeral Rites*, p. 33.
76. *Ibid.*, p. 97.
77. Genet, *The Journal*, p. 22.
78. *Ibid.*, p. 206.
79. *Ibid.*, p. 208.
80. *Ibid.*, p. 211.
81. Genet, *Miracle*, p. 11.
82. *Ibid.*, p. 126.
83. Genet, *The Journal*, p. 209.
84. *Ibid.*, p. 208.
85. *Ibid.*, p. 213.
86. *Ibid.*, p. 205.
87. *Ibid.*, p. 209.
88. *Ibid.*, p. 215.
89. *Ibid.*, p. 211.
90. Genet, *Funeral Rites*, p. 80.
91. Genet, *Our Lady*, p. 109.
92. *Ibid.*, p. 305.
93. Genet, *Funeral Rites*, p. 107.
94. Genet, *Miracle*, p. 66.
95. Genet, *Our Lady*, p. 308.
96. Genet, *Miracle*, pp. 311–312.
97. Genet, *Funeral Rites*, p. 104.

98. Genet, *Miracle*, p. 342.
99. Genet, *Our Lady*, p. 280.
100. Genet, *Miracle*, pp. 29–31.
101. *Ibid.*, p. 198.
102. *Ibid.*, p. 130.
103. Genet, *Funeral Rites*, p. 80.
104. Genet, *The Journal*, p. 46.
105. Genet, *Funeral Rites*, p. 170.
106. Joseph Conrad, *Under Western Eyes*, Canterbury Ed. (Doubleday Doran & Company, Inc., 1924), Vol. XXII, p. 39.

6
Wrestlers with Christ and Cupid

1. Nathanael West, *Miss Lonelyhearts* (New Directions, 1945), p. 35.
2. *Ibid.*, p. 106.
3. *Ibid.*, p. 13.
4. *Ibid.*, p. 30.
5. *Ibid.*, p. 21.
6. *Ibid.*, p. 19.
7. *Ibid.*, p. 9.
8. *Ibid.*, pp. 10, 11.
9. *Ibid.*, p. 35.
10. *Ibid.*, p. 30.
11. *Ibid.*, p. 6.
12. *Ibid.*, p. 2.
13. *Ibid.*, p. 34.
14. *Ibid.*, p. 59.
15. Oscar Wilde, *The Works of Oscar Wilde: Poems*, "Ballad of Reading Gaol" (C. T. Brainard Co., 1909), p. 253.
16. West, *Miss Lonelyhearts*, p. 139.
17. *Ibid.*, p. 141.
18. Stanley Edgar Hyman, *Nathanael West* (University of Minnesota Press, 1962), pp. 22–23.
19. West, *Miss Lonelyhearts*, p. 40.
20. Ernest Hemingway, *The Sun Also Rises* (Charles Scribner's Sons, 1954), p. 20.
21. West, *Miss Lonelyhearts*, p. 28.
22. *Ibid.*, p. 30.
23. *Ibid.*, pp. 64, 65.
24. *Ibid.*, p. 13.
25. *Ibid.*, p. 66.
26. *Ibid.*, p. 50.

27. *Ibid.,* p. 51.
28. *Ibid.,* p. 56.
29. Hyman, *Nathanael West,* p. 23.
30. West, *Miss Lonelyhearts,* p. 57.
31. *Ibid.,* p. 117.
32. *Ibid.,* p. 120.
33. *Ibid.,* p. 140.
34. *Ibid.,* pp. 29, 30.
35. *Ibid.,* p. 134.
36. *Ibid.,* p. 35.
37. *Ibid.,* pp. 15, 16.
38. *Ibid.,* p. 21.
39. *Ibid.,* p. 78.
40. *Ibid.,* p. 83.
41. Flannery O'Connor, *Mystery and Manners,* ed. by Sally and Robert Fitzgerald (Farrar, Straus & Giroux, Inc., 1969), p. 202.
42. *Ibid.,* p. 197.
43. St. John of the Cross, *The Dark Night of the Soul,* tr. by Benedict Zimmerman (London: Thomas Baker, 1924), pp. 22–23.
44. O'Connor, *Mystery and Manners,* p. 132.
45. *Ibid.,* p. 207.
46. *Ibid.,* p. 209.
47. Flannery O'Connor, *Wise Blood* (Harcourt, Brace & Company, Inc., 1952), p. 20.
48. *Ibid.,* p. 110.
49. *Ibid.,* p. 30.
50. *Ibid.,* p. 34.
51. *Ibid.,* p. 110.
52. *Ibid.,* pp. 146–147.
53. *Ibid.,* p. 22.
54. *Ibid.,* p. 105.
55. *Ibid.,* p. 152.
56. *Ibid.,* p. 24.
57. *Ibid.,* pp. 140–141.
58. *Ibid.,* p. 48.
59. Stanley Edgar Hyman, *Flannery O'Connor* (University of Minnesota Press, 1966), pp. 9–10.
60. O'Connor, *Wise Blood,* p. 69.
61. *Ibid.,* p. 115.
62. O'Connor, *Mystery and Manners,* p. 72.
63. O'Connor, *Wise Blood,* p. 114.
64. *Ibid.,* p. 72.
65. *Ibid.,* p. 63.
66. *Ibid.,* p. 209.

67. *Ibid.*, p. 23.
68. O'Connor, *Mystery and Manners*, p. 164.
69. *Ibid.*, p. 72.
70. O'Connor, *Wise Blood*, p. 218.
71. *Ibid.*, p. 105.
72. O'Connor, *Mystery and Manners*, p. 32.
73. *Ibid.*, p. 112.
74. O'Connor, *Wise Blood*, p. 224.
75. *Ibid.*, p. 221.
76. Flannery O'Connor, *Everything That Rises Must Converge* (Farrar, Straus & Giroux, Inc., 1965), p. 235.
77. *Ibid.*, p. 244.
78. W. K. Wimsatt and M. C. Beardsley, *The Verbal Icon: Studies in the Meaning of Poetry* (University of Kentucky Press, 1954), p. 3.
79. O'Connor, *Mystery and Manners*, p. 83.
80. Flannery O'Connor, *The Violent Bear It Away* (Farrar, Straus & Cudahy, Inc., 1955), p. 242.
81. O'Connor, *Mystery and Manners*, p. 174.
82. *Ibid.*, p. 117.
83. Hyman, *Flannery O'Connor*, p. 23.
84. O'Connor, *Everything That Rises*, p. 184.
85. Hyman, *Flannery O'Connor*, pp. 32–33.
86. O'Connor, *Everything That Rises*, p. 238.
87. O'Connor, *Mystery and Manners*, p. 118.

7

The Sexy Cross

1. Very little of Léon Bloy's prodigious output has been translated into English, and little of the original French is available in the United States. For that reason, I have taken all the Bloy quotations in this chapter from Donat O'Donnell's *Maria Cross: Imaginative Patterns in a Group of Modern Catholic Writers* (Oxford University Press, 1952), pp. 203–222.
2. Paul Claudel, *The Satin Slipper*, tr. by John O'Connor (Yale University Press, 1931), p. 130.
3. François Mauriac, *The Little Misery*, tr. by Gerard Hopkins (London: Eyre and Spottiswoode, 1952), p. 106.
4. François Mauriac, *Commencements d'une vie* (Paris: Bernard Grasset, 1932), pp. 34–35.
5. Evelyn Waugh, *Black Mischief* (Little, Brown & Company, 1946), p. 237.
6. François Mauriac, *The Frontenacs*, tr. by Gerard Hopkins

(Farrar, Straus and Cudahy, Inc., 1961), p. 12.

7. Graham Greene, *Journey Without Maps* (London: William Heinemann, Ltd., 1950), p. 32.

8. Graham Greene, *The End of the Affair* (The Viking Press, Inc., 1951), p. 147.

9. Charles Péguy, "Jeanne d'Arc," *Oeuvres poétiques complètes* (Paris: Gallimard, 1948), p. 959.

10. Graham Greene, *A Burnt-Out Case* (The Viking Press, Inc., 1961), p. 3.

11. Péguy, "Jeanne d'Arc," p. 959.

12. Georges Bernanos, *Un Mauvais Rêve* (Paris: Plon, 1950), p. 188.

13. Georges Bernanos, *The Diary of a Country Priest*, tr. by Pamela Morris (Doubleday & Company, Inc., 1954), p. 9.

14. Georges Bernanos, *L'Imposture* (Paris: Plon, 1955), p. 183.

15. François Mauriac, *Souffrances et bonheur du Chrétien*, in *Oeuvres complètes* (Paris: Bernard Grasset, 1951), VII, p. 251.

16. François Mauriac, *The Desert of Love*, in *A Mauriac Reader*, tr. by Gerard Hopkins (Farrar, Straus & Giroux, Inc., 1968), p. 242.

17. Greene, *The End of the Affair*, p. 116.

18. Georges Bernanos, *The Star of Satan*, tr. by Pamela Morris (The Macmillan Company, 1940), p. 129.

19. Charles Péguy, "Prière de confidence," *Oeuvres poétiques complètes* (Paris: Gallimard, 1948), p. 698.

20. Graham Greene, *The Ministry of Fear*, in *3 by Graham Greene* (The Viking Press, Inc., 1952), p. 145.

21. Graham Greene, *The Lost Childhood* (The Viking Press, Inc., 1952), p. 16.

22. Evelyn Waugh, *A Little Learning* (London: Chapman and Hall, 1964), p. 196.

23. François Mauriac, *God and Mammon* (London: Sheed & Ward, Ltd., 1936), pp. 24–25.

24. Waugh, *A Little Learning*, p. 44.

25. *Ibid.*, p. 229.

26. Graham Greene, *A Sort of Life* (Simon & Schuster, Inc., 1971), p. 88.

27. Mauriac, *Souffrances et bonheur du Chrétien*, p. 229.

28. François Mauriac, *La vie de Jean Racine* (Paris: Plon, 1928), p. 47.

29. Seán O'Faoláin, "The Small Lady," *Midsummer Night Madness and Other Stories* (The Viking Press, Inc., 1932), p. 115.

30. Seán O'Faoláin, *Bird Alone* (The Viking Press, Inc., 1936), p. 72.

31. *Ibid.*, p. 280.

32. François Mauriac, *Woman of the Pharisees,* tr. by Gerard Hopkins (Henry Holt & Company, Inc., 1946), p. 140.
33. D. H. Lawrence, *Women in Love* (Modern Library, Inc., n.d.), p. 338.
34. Georges Bernanos, *Monsieur Ouine* (Paris: Plon, 1946), p. 212.
35. Bernanos, *L'Imposture,* p. 166.
36. G. K. Chesterton, *The Napoleon of Notting Hill* (The Devin-Adair Co., 1950), p. 164.
37. Charles Péguy, "Éve," *Oeuvres poétiques complètes* (Paris: Gallimard, 1948), p. 917.
38. Evelyn Waugh, *Scott-King's Modern Europe* (Little, Brown & Company, 1949), p. 89.
39. Evelyn Waugh, *Brideshead Revisited* (Dell Publishing Company, 1960), p. 98.
40. Mauriac, *The Frontenacs,* p. 10.

Conclusion

1. Sigmund Freud, *Civilization and Its Discontents,* tr. by Joan Riviere (Doubleday & Company, Anchor Book, n.d.), p. 58.
2. Quotation taken from "The Second Sexual Revolution," *Time,* Jan. 24, 1964, p. 56.
3. Golding, *The Spire,* p. 212.
4. Lawrence, *The Collected Letters,* p. 312.
5. Quotation taken from "View from the Catacombs," *Time,* April 26, 1968, p. 68.
6. John Updike, *Assorted Prose* (Alfred A. Knopf, Inc., 1965), p. 287.
7. Jean Genet, *Our Lady of the Flowers,* p. 152.
8. *Ibid.,* p. 158.
9. Jean Genet, *The Thief's Journal,* p. 261.
10. Nathanael West, *The Dream Life of Balso Snell* in *The Complete Works of Nathanael West* (Farrar, Straus and Cudahy, Inc., 1957), p. 10.
11. C. S. Lewis, *The Four Loves* (Harcourt, Brace and Company, Inc., 1960), pp. 11, 19, 178.
12. Thomas à Kempis, *The Following of Christ* (Thomas J. Flynn and Co., n.d.), p. 34.
13. Letter from Heloise to Abelard, tr. by J. T. Muckle, *Mediaeval Studies* (Toronto: The Pontifical Institute of Mediaeval Studies, 1953), Vol. XV, p. 62.
14. François Mauriac, *The Stumbling Block* (Philosophical Library, 1952), p. 10.
15. James Cleugh, *Love Locked Out* (London: Hamlyn House, 1970), p. 297.

16. C. G. Jung, *Two Essays on Analytical Psychology*, tr. by R. F. C. Hull (Pantheon Books, Inc.: Bollingen Series No. 20, 1953), p. 17, n. 8.
17. W. H. Auden, "An Odd Ball in an Odd Country at an Odd Time," *The New York Review of Books*, Nov. 1, 1973, p. 10.

Index

Abelard, Pierre, 174, 199
Aesthetes and Decadents of the 1890's (Beckson), 121n73, 194
Albright, William, 189
Allegro, John, 16–17, 185
Anchor Bible: The Acts of the Apostles, The (Munck), 78n6, 189
Aristophanes, 18
Art of Courtly Love, The (De Amore), 29, 186
Artaud, Antonin, 117
Assorted Prose (Updike), 171n6, 199
Auden, W. H., 183, 200
Augustine, 23, 30, 175

Balcony, The (Genet), 172
Barth, Karl, 170–171
Basic Writings of St. Augustine, 30, 186
Battaglia, S., 186
Baudelaire, Charles, 123, 142–143
Beardsley, M. C., 151, 197
Beckson, Karl, 194
Bernanos, Georges, 157, 161, 162, 165–167, 175, 198, 199
Bernard, St., 183

Bird Alone (O'Faoláin), 163–164nn30, 31; 198
Black Mischief (Waugh), 159, 197
Blatty, Peter, 25
Bloy, Léon, 157–158, 160–161, 162, 165, 166, 167, 175, 197
Brewster, Earl, 38
Brideshead Revisited (Waugh), 166–167, 199
Brighton Rock (Greene), 142, 160, 165–166
Burnt-Out Case, A (Greene), 160, 198
Byron, Lord, 114

Calvin, John, 171
Camino Real (Williams), 100, 103, 191
Camus, Albert, 80
Capellanus, Andreas, 29, 186
Carmina Burana, 30–31, 186
Catullus, 31, 177
Centaur, The (Updike), 170–171
Chansons de Jaufré Rudel, Les, 30, 186
Chaucer, Geoffrey, 164
Chesterton, G. K., 110, 157, 165, 167, 175, 199

Civilization and Its Discontents (Freud), 169, 199

Claudel, Paul, 157–158, 160, 164, 166–167, 175, 178, 197

Clement of Alexandria, 24

Cleugh, James, 25, 177, 186, 199

Cole, William, 18, 20, 185

Collected Letters of D. H. Lawrence, The, 37–57, 170, 186–188, 199

Commencements d'une vie (Mauriac), 158, 197

Complete Works of Friedrich Nietzsche, The, 102, 192

Conrad, Joseph, 128, 195

Cool Million, A (N. West), 174

Cooper, J. S., 17, 185

Coover, Robert, 185

Couples (Updike), 75, 80, 82–98, 171, 190–191

Crashaw, Richard, 33

Cruelest Month, The (Wilhelm), 31, 186

Damian, Peter, 183

Dante, 33, 96, 110

Dark Night of the Soul, The (St. John of the Cross), 140, 196

Death of God, The (Vahanian), 102

Descartes, René, 122, 160

Desert of Love, The (Mauriac), 158, 161, 198

Devil's Advocate, The (M. West), 178–179

Diary of a Country Priest, The (Bernanos), 161, 198

Dostoevsky, Fyodor, 37, 42, 80

Douglas, Lord Alfred, 121

Dream Life of Balso Snell, The (N. West), 173, 199

Edman, Irwin, 185

Eliot, T. S., 54, 143

End of the Affair, The (Greene), 159–160, 162, 198

Escaped Cock, The (Lawrence), 38–39

Everything That Rises Must Converge (F. O'Connor), 151, 155–156, 197

Exorcist, The (Blatty), 25

Faulkner, William, 136

Firbank, Ronald, 116

Fitzgerald, F. Scott, 132

Flannery O'Connor (Hyman), 144, 154–155, 196–197

Following of Christ, The (Thomas à Kempis), 174, 199

Forster, E. M., 42–43

Four Loves, The (Lewis), 174, 199

France, Anatole, 123

Frechtman, Bernard, 192–193

Freud, Sigmund, 59, 81, 87, 95, 136, 169, 174, 179

Frontenacs, The (Mauriac), 159

Funeral Rites (Genet), 113, 115, 117, 119–122, 125–127, 172, 193–195

Gass, William, 56–57, 188

Gavriiliada (Pushkin), 33

Genet, Jean, 14, 107–128, 137, 171–172, 176–179, 192–195, 199

Gnädiges Fräulein, The (Williams), 102, 104, 192

God and Mammon (Mauriac), 163, 198

Godley, A. D., 185

Goethe, Johann von, 33

Golden Bough, The (Frazer), 18

Golding, William, 57–58, 62, 66, 69–70, 74, 170, 176, 178, 188–189, 199

Gospel According to Luke, The (Stoll), 79n8, 189

Greeley, Andrew, 15, 185

Greene, Graham, 14, 90, 93, 132, 135, 142, 157, 159–167, 175, 178, 198
Gregorius, 183

Hegel, Georg, 102
Helena (Waugh), 159
Heloise, 174, 199
Hemingway, Ernest, 80, 134, 195
Herodotus, 18, 185
Hitler, Adolf, 118, 122–123
Hopkins, Gerard, 197–198
Hopkins, G. M., 66, 114
Hull, R. F. C., 200
Huysmans, Joris Karl, 129
Hyman, Stanley Edgar, 133, 135–136, 144, 154–155, 195–197

Ibsen, Henrik, 70–71, 189
Imposture, L' (Bernanos), 161, 165, 198–199
In the Bar of a Tokyo Hotel (Williams), 107

Jeanroy, A., 186
Jerome, 24
Jesus Rediscovered (Muggeridge), 13, 185
John of the Cross, St., 140, 196
John the Evangelist, 44, 140
Journey Without Maps (Greene), 159
Joyce, James, 34, 103, 135
Jung, C. S., 56, 180, 200

Keats, John, 66–67, 175
Kennedy, Eugene, 23, 185
Kingdom of Earth (Williams), 99, 103, 191
Kiss Sacred and Profane, The (Perella), 19, 21, 29, 31, 185, 186
Krafft-Ebing, Richard, 157

Laing, R. D., 131
Lawrence, D. H., 34–35, 37–57, 96, 119, 135, 164, 169–170, 174, 176, 178, 186–188, 199
Levy, Oscar, 192
Lewis, C. S., 174, 199
Little Learning, A (Waugh), 162, 163, 166, 198
Little Misery, The (Mauriac), 158, 197
Lost Childhood, The (Greene), 162, 198
Love Declared (Rougemont), 181
Love in the Western World (Rougemont), 167, 171, 181
Love Locked Out (Cleugh), 24–26, 177, 186, 199
Loved One, The (Waugh), 159
Luke, 78–79
Luther, Martin, 181

Magic Mountain, The (T. Mann), 77
Major Critical Essays (Shaw), 71, 189
Man and Superman (Shaw), 50, 187
Man Who Died, The (Lawrence), 37–57, 169, 186–188
Man Who Was Thursday, The (Chesterton), 110
Mann, C. S., 189
Mansfield, Katherine, 42, 51, 57
Maria Cross (O'Donnell), 197
Mark, 49
Martin, Jay, 173
Master Builder, The (Ibsen), 70–74, 189
Matthew, 22, 149
Maupassant, Guy de, 51
Mauriac, François, 157–159, 161, 163–164, 167, 175–176, 197–199

Mauvais Rêve, Un (Bernanos), 161, 198

Midsummer Night Madness (O'Faoláin), 163, 198

Milk Train Doesn't Stop Here Anymore, The (Williams), 101, 104, 172, 192

Milton, John, 95, 123

Ministry of Fear, The (Greene), 162, 198

Miracle of the Rose, The (Genet), 109–110, 112, 114–117, 119, 123, 125–127, 137, 192–195

Miss Lonelyhearts (N. West), 130–139, 142, 173–174, 195–196

Monsieur Ouine (Bernanos), 165, 199

Moore, Harry T., 37–38, 186

Morris, Pamela, 198

Muckle, J. T., 199

Muggeridge, Malcolm, 13, 185

Munck, Johannes, 189

Murry, Middleton, 42, 44

Mystery and Manners (F. O'Connor), 139–141, 145–146, 148–149, 152–153, 156, 196–197

Napoleon of Notting Hill, The (Chesterton), 165, 199

Nichols, Lewis, 189–191

Nicholson, R. A., 31, 186

Nietzsche, Friedrich, 23, 102, 113, 125, 192

Night of the Iguana, The (Williams), 101, 103, 172–173, 192

Nouvelle Héloïse, La (Rousseau), 33

Nygren, Anders, 181

Oates, Whitney J., 186

O'Connor, Flannery, 128–129, 139–141, 146, 148–153, 155–156, 173–174, 176, 178–179, 196–197

O'Connor, John, 197

O'Donnell, Donat, 197

Oeuvres poétiques complètes (Péguy), 160, 162, 165, 198, 199

O'Faoláin, Seán, 157, 163, 167, 175, 198

Orient Express (Greene), 159

Origen, 24

Orpheus Descending (Williams), 104, 192

Our Lady of the Flowers (Genet), 110–113, 115–121, 125–126, 171–172, 199

Ovid, 31

Pascal, Blaise, 161, 163, 165, 172, 175

Path Through Genesis, The (Vawter), 84n28, 190

Paul, 19–21, 23, 180–181

Péguy, Charles, 157, 160, 162, 165–167, 175, 198, 199

Perella, Nicholas, 19, 21, 29, 31, 33, 185, 186

Peter, 17, 54, 131

Phipps, William, 21, 185

Plato, 18–19n10, 185

Poorhouse Fair, The (Updike), 75–83, 97, 189

Power and the Glory, The (Greene), 162, 165–166

Prudentius, 31

Pushkin, Alexander, 33

Rabbit, Run (Updike), 171

Racine, Jean, 163, 198

Rainbow, The (Lawrence), 35, 39, 48, 55–56, 186–188

Rimbaud, Arthur, 119

Riviere, Joan, 199

Robinson, E. A., 100

Rougemont, Denis de, 167, 171, 181

Rousseau, Jean Jacques, 33
Rudel, Jaufré, 30, 186
Russell, Bertrand, 42

Sacred Mushroom and the Cross, The (Allegro), 16–17, 185
Sade, Marquis de, 111, 157
Saint Genet (Sartre), 112–113, 116, 125, 193
Salimbene di Adamo, 25
Sappho, 31
Sartre, Jean-Paul, 115–116, 125, 193
Satin Slipper, The (Claudel), 158, 197
Schopenhauer, Arthur, 179
Scott-King's Modern Europe (Waugh), 166, 199
Selected Essays (Troy), 40, 186
Sex and Love in the Bible (Cole), 18, 20, 185
Shaw, Bernard, 50, 71, 187, 189
Shelley, Percy, 114
Small Craft Warnings (Williams), 99, 107
Solovyev, Vladimir, 172
Sons and Lovers (Lawrence), 52–53
Sorrows of Young Werther, The (Goethe), 33
Sort of Life, A (Greene), 163, 198
Souffrances et bonheur du Chrétien (Mauriac), 161, 163, 198
Spire, The (Golding), 58–74, 170, 188–189
Star of Satan, The (Bernanos), 162, 198
Stoll, Raymond F., 79, 189
Studies in Islamic Mysticism (Nicholson), 31, 186
Stumbling Block, The (Mauriac), 176, 199

Suddenly Last Summer (Williams), 99–100, 103, 172, 191–192
Summer and Smoke (Williams), 100, 172, 191
Sun Also Rises, The (Hemingway), 135
Sweet Bird of Youth (Williams), 100–101, 103–104, 172, 192
Symposium (Plato), 18

Teresa of Ávila, 32–33, 183
Tertullian, 24
Thief's Journal, The (Genet), 108–109, 111–116, 118–120, 122–124, 127, 172, 192, 193, 194, 195, 199
This Gun for Hire (Greene), 159
Thomas à Kempis, 108, 174, 199
Thomas, Dylan, 88, 93
Troy, William, 40, 186
Two Essays on Analytical Psychology (Jung), 180, 200

Under Western Eyes (Conrad), 128, 195
Updike, John, 74–75, 77–83, 86–87, 93–94, 97–98, 139, 170–171, 176, 178, 189–191, 199

Vahanian, Gabriel, 102
Vawter, Bruce, 84n28, 190
Verbal Icon, The (Wimsatt), 151, 197
Vie de Jean Racine, La (Mauriac), 163, 198
Vincent de Paul, 124
Violent Bear It Away, The (F. O'Connor), 141, 149, 152–154, 156, 197

Was Jesus Married? (Phipps), 21, 185
Waugh, Evelyn, 157, 159, 161–

163, 166–167, 175, 197, 198, 199
Weekley, Frieda, 50–54, 56
Wells, H. G., 34
West, Morris, 178–179
West, Nathanael, 128–131, 137, 139, 155–156, 173–174, 176, 178, 195–196, 199
Wilde, Oscar, 121, 132, 195
Wilhelm, James, 31, 186
William of Aquitaine, 29
Williams, Tennessee, 98–107, 172–173, 176, 191–192
Wimsatt, W. K., 151, 197

Wise Blood (F. O'Connor), 141–152, 196–197
Woman of the Pharisees (Mauriac), 164, 199
Women in Love (Lawrence), 164, 199
Works of Oscar Wilde, The, 132, 195

Yeats, W. B., 44, 154

Zimmerman, Benedict, 140n43, 196